The best of
NAMIBIA

WILLIE & SANDRA OLIVIER

NEW
HOLLAND

GLOBETROTTER™

First edition published in 2004
by New Holland Publishers (UK) Ltd
London • Cape Town • Sydney • Auckland
10 9 8 7 6 5 4 3 2

website: www.newhollandpublishers.com

Garfield House, 86 Edgware Road
London W2 2EA
United Kingdom

80 McKenzie Street
Cape Town 8001
South Africa

Unit 1, 66 Gibbes Street,
Chatswood, NSW 2067
Australia

218 Lake Road
Northcote, Auckland
New Zealand

Distributed in the USA by
The Globe Pequot Press, Connecticut

ISBN 978 1 84330 618 4

Although every effort has been made to ensure
that this guide is up to date and current at time
of going to print, the Publisher accepts no
responsibility or liability for any loss, injury or
inconvenience incurred by readers or travellers
using this guide.

Publishing Manager: Thea Grobbelaar
DTP Cartographic Manager: Genené Hart
Editor: Melany McCallum
Designer: Lellyn Creamer
Cover design: Lellyn Creamer, Nicole Bannister
Cartographer: Nicole Bannister
Picture Researcher: Shavonne Govender
Proofreader: Thea Grobbelaar

Reproduction by Fairstep (Cape Town) and
Hirt & Carter (Pty) Ltd, Cape Town
Printed and bound in by Times Offset (M) Sdn.
Bhd., Malaysia

Photographic Credits:
ABPL/Peter Tarr: page 6;
Gerald Cubitt: pages 11, 14, 16, 26, 28, 31,
34, 36, 41, 46, 49, 51, 53, 54, 56, 66, 68, 69,
76, 81;
Roger de la Harpe: page 13;
Jéan du Plessis: pages 8, 10, 17, 40, 58, 78;
Johan Jooste: page 7;
Johan Kloppers: page 15;
Willie and Sandra Oliver: pages 18, 19, 21,
22, 23, 24, 25, 29, 32, 33, 38, 39, 42, 44. 45,
47, 50, 57, 70, 74, 75, 80, 84;
Photo Access/Joe Brooks: page 20;
David Rogers: page 83;
Peter Steyn: page 27;
IOA: page 67;
IOA/Walter Knirr: page 43;
IOA/Peter Pickford: title page;
Mark van Aardt: pages 48, 52;
Friedrich von Hörsten: page 35;
Hein von Hörsten: page 30;
Patrick Wagner: cover.
[IOA: Struik Image Library]

Front Cover: *The sweeping dunes at Sossusvlei
dwarf a vehicle in the foreground.*
Title Page: *In Kaokoland, this graceful Himba
woman walks proudly in her traditional dress
and adornments.*

CONTENTS

⊕ USING THIS BOOK   4

🅟 OVERVIEW   6
The Land   6
History in Brief   7
Economy   9
The People   10

🌐 HIGHLIGHTS   14
Etosha National Park   14
Sesriem and Sossusvlei   15
Fish River Canyon   16
Windhoek   17
Namib Section of Namib-
    Naukluft Park   18
Swakopmund   19
Twyfelfontein   20
Cape Cross   21
Lüderitz   22
Waterberg Plateau Park   23
Naukluft   24
Duwisib Castle   25
Walvis Bay   26
Skeleton Coast   27
Southern Kaokoland   28
Northern Kaokoland   29
Spitzkoppe   30
Caprivi   31
Hoba Meteorite   32
Quiver Tree Forests   33

📷 SIGHTSEEING   34
Land of Contrasts   34
Historic Buildings   36
Places of Worship   37
Museums   37
Parks and Gardens   40

🌼 ACTIVITIES   41
Sport and Recreation   41
Adventure Activities   42

Fun For Children   46
Namibia From the Air   47
Walking Tours   48
Organized Tours   52

🛍 SHOPPING   54
Shopping in Windhoek   54
Shopping in
    Swakopmund   55
Craft Markets   56

🏠 ACCOMMODATION   58
Where to Stay   58

🍴 EATING OUT   66
What to Eat   66
What to Drink   68
Where to Eat   71

🎭 ENTERTAINMENT   74
Nightlife   74
Music and Theatre   74
Gambling   75
Spectator Sports   76
Nightclubs, Bars &
    Discos   77

🚌 EXCURSIONS   78
The Desert Express   79
Canoeing the Orange
    River   80
Camel Safaris   81
Namib Horse Trails   82
Botswana and
    Zimbabwe   82

❄ TRAVEL TIPS   84

INDEX OF SIGHTS   92

GENERAL INDEX   93

MAKE THE MOST OF YOUR GUIDE

Reading these two pages will help you to get the most out of your guide and save you time when using it. Sites discussed in the text are cross-referenced with the cover maps – for example, the reference 'Map A–C3' refers to the Southern Namibia Map (Map A), column C, row 3. Use the Map Plan below to quickly locate the map you need.

MAP PLAN

Outside Back Cover

Outside Front Cover

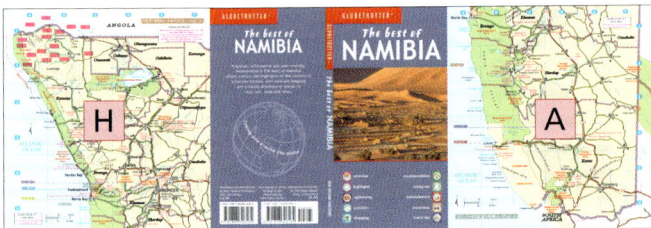

Inside Front Cover

Inside Back Cover

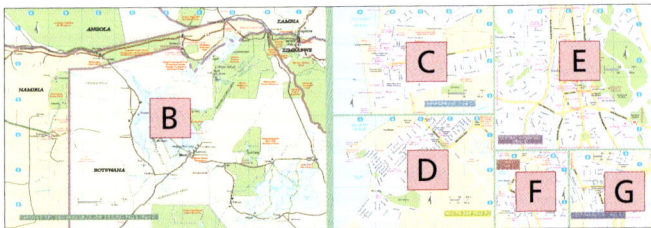

THE BIGGER PICTURE

Key to the Map Plan

A – Southern Namibia
B – Caprivi Strip, Okavango Delta and Victoria Falls
C – Swakopmund
D – Walvis Bay
E – Central Windhoek
F – Lüderitz
G – Keetmanshoop
H – Northern Namibia

USING THIS BOOK

Please Note

Mail is not delivered to street addresses. These are provided to locate places, rather than to contact them by mail.

Key to Symbols

⊠ — address
☎ — telephone
🖂 — fax
🖳 — website
🖰 — e-mail
🕐 — opening times
🚌 — tour
💰 — entry fee
🍴 — restaurants

Map Legend

national road		main road	**Fidel Castro**
main road		other road	Bismarck
minor road		mall	**MALL**
track		built-up area	
4x4 track		viewpoint	
other road		place of interest	● State House
railway		hotel	Ⓗ STEINER
river		lodge	Ⓛ CAÑON LODGE
route number	B1	rest camp/ guest farm	Ai-Ais
city	WINDHOEK	luxury tented camp	▲
major town	◉ Otavi	camp site	▵
town	O Rehoboth	parking area	P
large village	◎ Tses	building of interest	Owela Museum
village	O Warmquelle	library	
airport		post office	⊠
airfield	✈	tourist information	i
golf course		place of worship	△
mountain peak	Brukkaros ▲ 1586 m	police station	●
GPS co-ordiantes	18°03′29″S 13°15′31″E	bus terminus	
petrol station		hospital	⊕
waterfall/swamp			
cave			
park & garden	*Etosha National Park*		

Keep us Current

Travel information is apt to change, which is why we regularly update our guides. We'd be most grateful to receive feedback from you if you've noted something we should include in our updates. If you have any new information, please share it with us by writing to the Publishing Manager, Globetrotter, at the office nearest to you (addresses on the imprint page of this guide). The most significant contribution to each new edition will be rewarded with a free copy of the updated guide.

Above: *Sandwich Harbour is a haven for migratory shorebirds.*

Fauna
Namibia has the largest populations of the western subspecies of the **black rhino** and **cheetah** in the world. It also has healthy populations of **elephant**, **lion** and **leopard**, as well as rare species such as **black-faced impala** and **roan**. The **gemsbok** (oryx), the national animal, and **springbok** are hardy desert inhabitants. **Kudu** (antelope with magnificent spiral horns) occur widely, while **red lechwe**, **sitatunga**, **oribi** and **waterbuck** only occur in the northeast. The northern rivers are home to **crocodile** and **hippo**. **Hartmann's mountain zebra** inhabit the mountainous escarpment in the west of the country and, except for a small population in southwestern Angola, they are confined to Namibia.

NAMIBIA

Namibia, a country of striking contrasts, vast open spaces, awesome landscapes and a blend of ancient cultures, is situated in the southwestern corner of Africa. Bounded in the north by Angola and Zambia, it stretches southwards for over 1300km (800 miles) to the Orange (Gariep) River, which forms its southern boundary with South Africa. At its widest, it extends for 1440km (900 miles) from the Skeleton Coast eastwards to Impalila Island where the boundaries of Namibia converge with those of Zambia, Zimbabwe and Botswana. In the west the Atlantic Ocean forms a natural boundary for almost 1600km (1000 miles), while Botswana and South Africa are to its east.

The Land
Climate

With over 300 sunny days a year, Namibia is a land of sunshine and clear blue skies. It is the most arid country in sub-Saharan Africa with an average annual rainfall of only 270mm (10.6in). Summer rain is the norm, but is highly unpredictable. Temperatures are generally pleasant, but drop to below 5°C (41°F) in winter, while in midsummer they soar above 30°C (86°F).

Flora

The vegetation ranges from hardy desert grasses and bushes in the west to dense woodlands in the north and northeast. The most famous plant is the desert-adapted *Welwitschia mirabilis* which is endemic to the Namib Desert. The southwestern corner of the country is home to a rich diversity of rare aloes and other succulents.

History in Brief
Pre-colonial Times

The San, or Bushmen, descendants of the Later Stone Age people, were the first known inhabitants of Namibia. Living in small bands throughout the country, they pursued a highly mobile lifestyle and existed from the hunting of animals and the gathering of veld foods.

Between 2000 and 3000 years ago the Nama, a subgroup of the Khoikhoi, migrated into the southern reaches of Namibia. They brought fat-tailed sheep with them, and later aquired cattle and goats from the Tswana who lived to the east. Their pastoral mode of existence was supplemented with hunting and gathering. From southern Namibia they extended their territory to the central parts of the country.

Early Explorers and Colonialism

The first European to set foot on Namibian soil was the Portuguese navigator Diego Cão who planted a cross at Cape Cross, 120km (75 miles) north of Swakopmund, in 1486. The inhospitable coastline and interior, however, served as an effective deterrent against colonization for over four centuries.

Following the European powers' Scramble for Africa and the annexation of the Walvis Bay enclave by Great Britain in 1878, a German protectorate was declared over Lüderitz and its surroundings in 1884. German colonial rule was gradually extended over the rest of the country and Namibians were systematically dispossessed of their land. In 1890 Germany declared its protectorate a crown colony.

Early Rock Art
The oldest evidence of artistic expression in Namibia was first discovered in a cave in southern Namibia in 1969. The excavation coincided with the return of Apollo 11 and archaeologist Dr Erik Wendt named the cave after the mission. Fragments of flat stone with paintings were excavated from the cave and in 1972 a painted fragment was discovered that fitted one that was unearthed in 1969. Radiocarbon dating of the deposits in which the painted slabs were discovered put their age at between 25,000 and 28,000 years. Paintings on flat stones, rather than fixed surfaces, are known as mobile art or *art mobilier*.

Below: *A member of Namibia's Baster community. Her forefathers left the Cape in 1870 to settle in Namibia.*

Below: *The Rider Memorial (1912) in Windhoek honours German soldiers killed in the 1903–07 Nama and Herero wars.*

Resistance

The Witbooi Nama refused to submit to German rule and engaged the German *Schutztruppe* (territorial troops) in a war that lasted from April 1893 to August 1894. In October 1903 the Bondelswarts Nama rebelled in the far south of the country and on 11 January 1904 the Herero Chief, Samuel Maharero, gave the command for a general uprising. Several hundred Ndonga warriors attacked Fort Namutoni in the north of the country on 28 January.

The flames of war spread south when the Nama Chief Hendrik Witbooi declared war on 5 October 1904. Following Witbooi's death in October 1905, the war came to a gradual end, but sporadic guerrilla clashes continued until 1907.

South African forces invaded the then South West Africa soon after the outbreak of World War I. The German troops surrendered on 9 July 1915 and the territory subsequently became a mandate of South Africa. This heralded the beginning of a new chapter in the country's history.

After the National Party came to power in South Africa in 1948, its policy of apartheid was strictly enforced in Namibia. Eleven 'homelands' were created for the various indigenous groups. Residential areas and schools were segregated and mixed marriages prohibited.

Liberation Struggle and Independence

In 1961 the South West African People's Organization (Swapo) launched an armed struggle. The first clash between Swapo soldiers and the South African Police took place in northern Namibia on 26 August

1966. In the 23-year struggle that followed over 6800 Swapo fighters and members lost their lives while nearly 1000 were reported missing.

United Nations Resolution 435, which paved the way for independence, came into force on 1 April 1989. In November of that year Namibians went to the polls and Swapo won with 56.6% of the vote. Independence came on 21 March 1990 when the South African flag was lowered and Swapo leader Sam Nujoma was sworn in as Namibia's first president.

Above: *The Namibian Flag was first raised when Sam Nujoma was inaugurated as Namibia's first democratically elected president on 20 March 1990.*

Economy

Mining is the mainstay of the economy and accounted for 69% of exports in 2002 and 11% of the GDP between 1996 and 2001. Namibia is a major diamond producer, especially gem quality stones, and there are vast reserves of zinc in the south of the country. Uranium, copper and gold are other important minerals and metals.

The central parts of the country are suited to **cattle ranching**, while small stock is reared for meat and pelts in the south. Prolonged droughts have caused many farmers to turn to **game farming** and **tourism**. The contribution of **fishing** and **fish processing** has increased steadily since independence, but has been negatively affected by adverse marine conditions.

Namibia's **per capita income** (US$1916 in 1999) is one of the highest in Africa, but incomes are extremely unevenly distributed between black and white and urban and rural inhabitants. Average household incomes in urban areas are more than three times higher than in rural areas.

Government

Namibia is a multiparty democracy headed by an executive president who is elected by direct popular vote for a five-year term, while the 72-member National Assembly is elected on the basis of proportional representation, also for five years. The second house of Parliament, the National Council, has two representatives from each of the country's 13 regions.

Despite its violent and bloody history Namibia has enjoyed peace and stability since independence. This is largely due to the government's policies of **national reconcilliation** and **affirmative action** which aims to ensure the advancement of the previously disadvantaged majority.

The People

Namibia is a multicultural society where tradition and modern lifestyle often coexist. Herero women with their elaborate headdresses and traditional dresses walking alongside well-dressed businessmen are a common sight in the capital.

The largest cultural group, the Owambo, live mainly in the north of the country, as do the Kavango and Caprivian people. Other cultural groups are the Damara, Herero, Nama, Coloureds and Rehoboth Basters. The Whites are mainly of German and Afrikaner origin, while the Tswana, the smallest population group, live in the extreme east of the country.

The pastoral Himba of northwestern Namibia and the Ju/'hoan San or Bushmen of eastern Namibia still largely pursue their traditional way of life.

About 40% of the country's 1,8 million people is concentrated in urban areas. Population density ranges from one person per six square kilometres in the south to over 300 per square kilometre in the densely populated urban areas in the north.

Religion

Although about 90% of Namibians are Christian, ancestral worship is still widely practised, often alongside Christianity. The major denominations are Lutheran, Anglican, Catholic and Methodist. A variety of charismatic churches can be visited in the main towns.

Himba

The Himba, a group of Otjiherero-speakers, made Kaokoland their home some 250 years ago when their kin moved to the central parts of the country. Since they are pastoralists they are constantly on the move with their cattle in search of grazing and live in several semipermanent settlements throughout the region. Some have, however, been attracted to more permanent settlements such as Opuwo where they live in squalor.

The women's striking features are enhanced when they apply a paste of ochre and animal fat to their bodies which gives their skin a rich gleaming colour. The men are tall and thin and are sometimes compared to the Masaai of East Africa. In many ways they seem oblivious to the revolutionary changes that have taken place outside what they consider their world, and their culture is still strictly maintained.

Historical Commemorations

Okahandja, 70km (43 miles) north of Windhoek, is of great historic significance to the Red Flag Herero (followers of Maharero) and the Mbanderu (a group closely related to the Herero), who congregate in the town each year to pay homage to their forefathers.

Maharero Day, the largest of the two events, is held on the weekend before or after 26 August. It dates back to August 1923 when the remains of Chief Samuel Maharero, who died in exile in Botswana, were reinterred here.

On the Saturday, Herero from all over the country gather at the Commando House on the western outskirts of the town. Here the men, dressed in khaki uniforms and decorated in an assortment of medals, take part in a military parade. The women wear their traditional red dresses, black bodices embroidered with gold and silver brocade and striking red headdresses.

On the Sunday, the procession sets off on a 4km (2.5-mile) walk to the **Herero Chiefs' grave complex** which lies at the end of a pathway lined by palm trees. Buried here are Chiefs Tjamuaha, Maharero, Samuel Maharero and Friedrich Maharero. After filing past the graves, they move on to the graves of Chiefs **Hosea Kutako** and **Clemens Kapuoo**. Also buried here is Jonker Afrikaner, Chief of the Nama Afrikaners until his death in 1861.

The **Mbanderu** assemble in the town on the weekend before or on 11 June to pay homage to their slain leader Chief Kahimemua

Wika

WIKA (Windhoeker Karneval), the capital's major cultural event, is usually scheduled for April. A German-style carnival with a distinctly Namibian flavour, it has been held annually since 1953. Festivities begin on a Friday with the *Prinzenball* where the Carnival Prince and Princess are introduced. Saturday morning is the *Umzug*, a float procession through the city to the SKW Hall where revellers are greeted with *Stimmungsmusik*, beer and refreshments. Other events include the *Büttenabend*, an evening of satire and humorous commentary from speakers standing in a barrel; an international evening (when English is spoken); a childrens' carnival, and the *Maskenball* (Fancy Dress Ball). The final event is the *Ausklang*.

Opposite: *Himba women, Kaokoland.*
Below: *A mural in Katutura boldly expresses support for Sam Nujoma.*

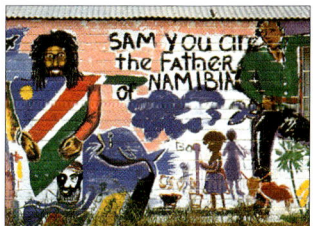

11

Nguvauva. He was executed by firing squad at Okahandja after a failed rebellion in June 1896 and buried in the town.

In **Omaruru**, the White Flag Herero commemorate **Zeraua Day** in the middle of October each year in deference to the ancestral Zeraua family.

Art on the Rocks

Namibia's art history dates back some 25,000 to 28,000 years (*see* panel, page 7). Best known among the hundreds of rock art sites is the **Brandberg** where early artists used boulders and caves as canvases to create an open-air gallery of over 44,000 paintings. The most famous of these is the so-called *White Lady* frieze in the Tsisab Ravine.

Where surfaces were not suitable for paintings, the early artists made delicate engravings into rock slabs. With over 2000 engravings, **Twyfelfontein**, (*see* page 20) has the highest concentration of rock engravings in Africa, but there are numerous other sites throughout the country.

Fine Art

Delicate pastel shades, wide-open spaces, landscapes and wildlife dominated the art scene from the early 1900s to the late 1960s. **Adolph Jentsch**, **Otto Scröder** and **Fritz Krampe** were the leading artists in this genre. Jentsch captured the spaciousness of the Namibian landscape in oils and watercolours, while Schröder's delicate pastels mainly portrayed the desert coast. Krampe's drawings of animals and birds conveyed a sense of action and movement.

John Muafangejo (*see* panel, this page), Namibia's best-known artist, pioneered the

Opposite: *Herero women display handcrafted dolls dressed in traditional garb.*

shift in subject matter from the landscape and wildlife tradition to black history and culture and the technique from painting to relief and intaglio printing.

Other well-known black Namibian artists include **Themba Masala, Peter Mwahalukange** and **Joseph Madisia**. The latter's linocut *Namibian Citizens* became famous during the run-up to Namibia's first democratic elections in 1989 when it was featured on T-shirts and posters.

Artistic Crafts

Embroidery, a craft taught by the wives of the German missionaries a century ago, was revived when the Lacheiner sisters initiated the **Ikhoba** project on a farm in the Otjiwarongo district in 1983 to improve the welfare of women on farms. Today about 400 women produce linen embroidered with colourful animal and ethnic designs for the project.

The **Anin** embroidery project was started by Heidi von Hase for women on a farm at Hoachanas in 1987 to enable them to earn an income. Anin means 'many birds' in the Nama language and birds feature prominently in the designs of the products.

At **Tikoloshe Afrika** in Omaruru, talented woodcarvers from the Kavango region in northern Namibia fashion exquisite **carvings** from roots of dead trees and weather-worn branches. Using their natural shape and texture, the roots and branches are transformed into a variety of animal sculptures.

Karakul Carpets and Rugs

Artistic talent has also found expression in innovative designs on karakul carpets, rugs and wall hangings which are hand-woven from karakul wool.

The industry began in 1952 when Ibenstein Weavers at Dordabis, a small farming settlement southeast of Windhoek, produced the first carpets.

Volker Berner of Dorka Teppiche, also in the Dordabis area, is internationally known for his high-quality carpets with their abstract and semi-abstract designs. An outstanding feature of the carpets is the blend of colours and tones – one carpet may have as many as 100 different hues. Hand-woven rugs and carpets with strong colours, earthy tints and a variety of designs are produced on the farm Kiripotib under the name Kirikara.

Above: *The water hole at Okaukuejo offers visitors a theatre-style view of wild animals.*

Moringa Forest

The Moringa Forest, an unusually dense concentration of moringa trees growing in the mopane-veld about 32km (20 miles) northwest of Okaukuejo rest camp, is one of the sights worth seeing. It is not only the large number of trees that makes the 'forest' unique, but the fact that the moringa tree usually grows on rocky mountain slopes and hillsides. The stunted and gnarled branches, and the fact that many trees have several trunks, add to the intrigue and have given rise to the name Fairy-tale Forest. Browsing of their tender shoots by elephant, giraffe and gemsbok is the cause of their weird shape and caused the park management to close some of the nearby waterholes in the 1980s to reduce the pressure on the trees.

🌼 *See* Map H–D2   ★★★

ETOSHA NATIONAL PARK

Namibia's flagship national park owes its name to the pan which covers nearly 25% of the park surface. Proclaimed in 1907, Etosha is a sanctuary to 114 mammal species including large numbers of elephant and black rhino. Burchell's zebra, blue wildebeest, spring-bok and gemsbok congregrate on the grasslands surrounding the pan, while the woodlands are home to herds of giraffe, red hartebeest, eland and black-faced impala. A wide variety of cats are represented, as well as a host of small mammals.

Since many of the water holes are situated in the open on the edge of the pan, game-viewing is much easier than in the more densely wooded parks elsewhere in southern Africa. In addition, the water holes on the perimeter of all three camps offer superb game-viewing, especially at night when they are floodlit.

Bird life is prolific and black-faced babbler, Monteiro's hornbill, Carp's tit and violet wood-hoopoe are noteworthy among the more than 340 species. The pan is one of only two regular breeding grounds of lesser and greater flamingo in southern Africa, attracting over a million when conditions are favourable.

The historic fort (1906) forms the focal point of **Namutoni** in the east, while **Halali** nestles amid shady mopane woodlands. A limestone water tower in **Okaukuejo**, the westernmost rest camp, provides a superb vantage point at sunset.

⬡ *See* Map A–B2

★★★

SESRIEM AND SOSSUSVLEI

A walk into **Sesriem Canyon**, about 4km (2.5 miles) south of Sesriem camp site, takes you back into history some 15–18 million years ago. The different sizes of the stones and the thickness of the various layers clearly indicate the intensity with which the ancient rivers flowed. The layers were later cemented into conglomerate and exposed when the canyon was eroded some two to four million years ago.

Sesriem is the gateway to **Sossusvlei**, a seemingly lost pan with a greyish-white mud-cracked floor that contrasts sharply with the spectacular high orange dunes surrounding it. The pan was formed when the great dunes of the Namib sand sea smothered the course of the Tsauchab River, some 60km (37 miles) east of the Atlantic Ocean. Years may go by before the river floods strongly enough to reach the pan, but when this happens Sossusvlei can hold water for up to a year.

Sossusvlei is best viewed just after sunrise when the sinuous orange crests of the dunes create dark shadows and abstract patterns. All but the last 5km (3 miles) of the 65km (40-mile) drive to the vlei is on tar. If you do not have a four-wheel-drive vehicle to drive the sandy track to the vlei you can walk, but make sure that you have water and suitable footwear.

!Nara and Dead Vlei
Although Sossusvlei is the best known pan, several others in the area are well worth exploring. On the rare occasions when the Tsauchab floods strongly enough to fill Sossusvlei, the spillover is diverted into the adjacent **!Naravlei**. The pan is named after the abundance of !nara plants which grow on the edge of the pan.

The **Dead Vlei**, with its shimmering white clay floor and bleached tree skeletons, presents a picture of utter devastation, reminiscent of an atomic explosion. Dating of the dead camelthorn trees indicates that it was cut off from the Tsauchab River's course some 500 years ago and subsequently became surrounded by dunes. The start of the 1.1km (0.7-mile) walk through loose sand is indicated a short way before you reach Sossusvlei.

Below: *The searing sands at Sossusvlei.*

See Map A–D5 ★★★

FISH RIVER CANYON

The formation of the Fish River Canyon dates back some 350 million years when a valley subsided along fault lines to form the upper floor of the canyon. The gentle southward slope of the land caused the Fish River to meander southwards and over millions of years it has gouged deeply into the ancient rocks to form the lower canyon.

Although the canyon is some 160km (100 miles) long, the most spectacular section stretches from just north of the northernmost viewpoint downstream for 65km (40 miles). The canyon is up to 27km (17 miles) wide and has a maximum depth of 549m (1801ft). Vantage points on the edge of the canyon provide awesome views of the sheer cliffs and raw beauty of the canyon. **Hobas camp site** is conveniently close to the canyon for those wanting to see the canyon at its best – at sunrise or just before sunset.

Those wanting to experience the canyon first-hand can tackle the **Fish River Canyon Hiking Trail** (see page 42) and follow its winding course for 85km (53 miles) from the northernmost lookout point to Ai-Ais (see panel). The hike (⊕ 15 Apr – 15 Sep) takes four to five days and hikers must be totally self-sufficient as there are no facilities.

Ai-Ais

Ai-Ais, 80km (50 miles) south of the main viewpoint overlooking the Fish River Canyon, is a Nama word which means 'scalding hot'. The name refers to the temperature of the thermal spring which, at 60°C (140°F), is one of the hottest in southern Africa. The water is rich in fluorides, chlorides and sulphates and is said to have a therapeutic effect on rheumatism and other ailments.

Built on the banks of the Fish River in a setting reminiscent of a moon landscape, the **Ai-Ais Resort** has an outdoor swimming pool (the water is cooled), an indoor spa complex and a variety of accommodation options ranging from luxury flats to camping sites with communal ablutions.

Tourism Office

Southern Tourist Forum
☎ (064) 22-1266

Right: *The Fish River gently wends its way through the craggy splendour of the canyon it has helped form.*

See Map E ★★

WINDHOEK

Nestling among the rolling hills of the central highlands, Windhoek is an attractive city where African and Western cultures meet in perfect harmony. German colonial buildings and modern multistorey buildings stand side by side along the city's main street, while pavement cafés create a continental atmosphere.

Above: *The landmark Christuskirche overlooks the city.*

People have been attracted to the hotwater springs in the valleys for thousands of years. In pre-colonial times they were known to the Nama as *Ai-//gams*, while the Herero referred to them as *Otjomuise*.

The abundance of water and the central location of the springs no doubt played a role in the decision to establish the headquarters of the German colonial administration here in 1890. Many **buildings** from the early 1900s (*see* pages 48–49) serve as a reminder of the country's early history.

The **TransNamib Museum**, **Owela Museum** and the **National Art Gallery of Namibia** cater for those interested in history, natural history and the arts (*see* pages 38–39).

Katutura, a sprawling suburb to the northwest of the city, is an interesting mixture of simple houses, luxurious residences and ever-expanding informal settlements, built in 'Blocks' for the different population groups during the apartheid years. It dates back to 1959 when residents of the 'Old Location', on the western outskirts of Windhoek, were forcefully moved to Katutura, a name meaning 'we have no dwelling place'.

Heroes' Acre
The Heroes' Acre, south of Windhoek, was unveiled in 2002 as a memorial to those who sacrificed their lives in the struggle against colonialism. There is a large obelisk which represents a sword (a symbol of strength, bravery and dedication), a Statue of the Unknown Soldier and a symbolic grave. The history of Namibia is depicted on a carved relief. Nine symbolic graves have been dedicated to early resistance fighters while 165 other freedom fighters will be interred at the site.

Tourist Offices
✉ Post Street Mall
☎ (061) 290-2092
✉ corner Fidel Castro Street and Independence Avenue
☎ (061) 290-2058
💻 www.windhoekcc.org.na
🖑 cityinfo@windhoekcc.org.na

Above: *The welwitschia lives for over 1000 years and produces just two leaves, which tangle and tear in desert winds.*
Opposite: *The Damara Tower forms a backdrop to a modern shopping mall.*

The Welwitschia

The welwitschia (*Welwitschia mirabilis*) is endemic to the Namib, occurring from the Kuiseb River northwards into southwestern Angola. It is a botanical curiosity with characteristics of cone-bearing and flowering plants with the male and female plants growing separately. Although it appears to have numerous leaves, only two are produced, but they become shredded by the extremes of temperatures and the desert winds. The giant Husab welwitschia on the Welwitschia Plains is estimated to be over 1500 years old.

🌸 *See* Map H–C6   ★★

NAMIB SECTION OF NAMIB-NAUKLUFT PARK

Sparsely vegetated plains punctuated occasionally by large, granite *inselbergen*, or island mountains, characterize the Namib section of the Namib-Naukluft Park.

Springbok and gemsbok roam the plains, while ostriches congregate in large flocks. Hartmann's mountain zebra inhabit the rugged Swakop and Kuiseb river valleys which are also home to leopard. Other species to be seen are black-backed jackal, bat-eared fox and a fascinating variety of lizards, beetles and other small creatures.

The **Welwitschia Drive** is a self-guided journey of about 145km (90 miles) from Swakopmund and back. Lichens, desert-adapted plants (such as the welwitschia) and spectacular views over the 'Moon Landscape' in the Swakop River Valley are among the points of interest along the route.

Two walks are available for those keen to explore the desert on foot. The **Rock Sculpture Trail** meanders past fascinating rock formations and can be completed in three hours at a leisurely pace. The **Tinkas Nature Walk**, which leads past a desert spring and an interesting geological formation, takes four to five hours to complete.

A permit is not required to travel on the proclaimed roads that cut across the park, but is required to explore the park roads. It can be obtained from the **Namibia Wildlife Resorts** (*see* panel, page 35) in Windhoek and Swakopmund.

| See Map C | ★★ |

SWAKOPMUND

Squeezed between the Namib Desert and the ocean, this enchanting coastal town resembles a piece of Germany that somehow got left behind in Africa. Cafés with delicious German confectionary add to its continental atmosphere. Swakop, the name generally used by Namibians, becomes a hive of activity in December when many people flock to the coast to escape the heat of the interior.

Heading the list of architectural treasures is the **Old Railway Station** (*see* panel, page 51), **Woermann House** (*see* panel, page 50) and the **Kaiserliches Bezirksgericht**. Other buildings include the **Hohenzollern House**, the **lighthouse** and **Villa Wille**. A walk through the streets (*see* page 50) is the best way to enjoy the town's atmosphere and appreciate its architecture.

A glass tunnel at the **National Marine Aquarium** provides great close-up views of ragged-tooth sharks, stingrays and a variety of Atlantic Ocean fishes. Divers feed them on Tuesdays, Saturdays and Sundays.

A spectacular collection of minerals and gemstones can be viewed at the **Kristall Galerie.** The largest quartz crystal cluster in the world, which weighs a massive 14,100kg (31,090lb), is included in the collection.

A visit to the **Swakopmund Museum** (*see* page 37) with its outstanding ethnographic collection should not be missed.

The dunes to the south of Swakopmund offer a variety of exciting **adventure sports** (*see* page 43).

Swakopmund's Jetty
The 262m (287yd) jetty has been a Swakopmund landmark for over three-quarters of a century. It was originally planned to extend 640m (700yd) into the sea, but World War I brought construction to a standstill and it was never completed. For many years it served as a vantage spot for spectacular sunset views and for anglers to cast their lines from. However, the battering waves and corrosion by the sea air weakened its iron supports and the jetty had to be closed. In 1983 the inshore section was rehabilitated and it was reopened, but a few years ago it became unsafe once again and was sealed off.

Namib i Tourist Office
✉ corner of Sam Nujoma Avenue and Hendrik Witbooi Street, Swakopmund
☎ (064) 30-3129

See Map H–C4 ★★

The Organ Pipes and Burnt Mountain

The **Organ Pipes**, a wall of hexagonal dolerite pillars, lie in a small gorge to the left of the road to the Burnt Mountain. They were formed when a dolerite sheet intruded the shale some 120 million years ago and split into angular columns when the rocks cooled down and shrank. Subsequent erosion by a river exposed them.

The **Burnt Mountain** owes its name to the cinder-like heap of rock, course-grained sand and multicoloured rocks that create the impression that the mountain had been razed by a fire. Basaltic magma intruded the Karoo shales and limestone of the mountain some 120 million years ago and the intense heat caused the release of hydroxides and oxides and the change in the colour of the rocks.

TWYFELFONTEIN

At Twyfelfontein, San artists have used the flat surfaces of the sandstone rock slabs and boulders on the mountain slopes as their canvasses to create an open-air gallery of exquisite rock art.

The artists painstakingly chisselled and etched over 2400 images into the rocks, leaving behind the largest known concentration of rock engravings in Africa. Among the interesting engravings are a lion with an unusually long, L-shaped tail and with spoor (tracks) instead of paws; a rhino, and an abstract figure, dubbed the '*Flying Kudu*'. Different techniques, such as cutting the outline and chiselling away the rock and scratching only the outline, were used.

The most commonly depicted animals are giraffe (316), ostrich (283), zebra (175) and rhinoceros (144), while unidentifiable antelope account for almost a quarter of the engravings. Gemsbok and springbok are depicted in 67 and 34 engravings respectively, while there are 383 animal spoor. Abstract patterns, handprints, footprints and other engravings related to humans account for nearly 15% of the engravings.

Twyfelfontein is managed as a community tourism project and to ensure that the engravings are not defaced or damaged, a guide must accompany visitors. Camping is available nearby at the **Aba-Huab camp site** run by the local community.

See Map H–B5   ★★

Left: *The granite* padrão *at Cape Cross was placed here in 1895.* **Opposite:** *Some of the petroglyphs, or rock engravings, to be found among the boulders of the Twyfelfontein area.*

CAPE CROSS

In 1486 the Portuguese navigator, Diego Cão, became the first European to set foot on Namibian soil. The **limestone cross** or *padrão* that he planted on the rocky promontory served as a landmark for early navigators for over four centuries until it was relocated to Germany in January 1893. It was replaced with a granite cross in 1895 and in 1980 an authentic replica of Cão's cross was unveiled on the exact spot where the original *padrão* stood.

Cape Cross is one of the largest of the 16 breeding colonies of **Cape fur seals** along the Namib Coast. The population fluctuates between 80,000 and 260,000 and the seals can be observed at close quarters from behind a low stone wall. Activity at the colony increases from mid-October when the bulls establish their territories. Most of the cows give birth from around the end of November to early December.

Cape Cross is open daily and permits can be obtained on arrival. Picnic facilities are available, but the duration of your stay will largely be dictated by the direction of the wind and the pungent smell of the seals. Alternatively, you can enjoy a light snack or meal at the adjacent Cape Cross Lodge.

Cape Fur Seal
The Cape fur seal is the only one of southern Africa's three species of fur seals that breeds in the subcontinent. The name 'fur seal' is used to distinguish it from the family of true seals. The average female weighs 75kg (165lb), while bulls have an average body mass of 187kg (412lb) which can increase to 360kg (794lb) just before the start of the rut. Fish account for 70% of their diet, followed by squid, octopus and cuttlefish (20%). Crustaceans and miscellaneous matter make up the remainder. The Cape fur seal can remain underwater for up to seven minutes and dive to depths of up to 200m (650ft).

Above: *Goerke House is a prime example of colonial architecture.*

Kolmanskop
At Kolmanskop, 10km (6 miles) east of Lüderitz, the shifting dunes, fierce winds and salt-laden mist have turned the once-thriving diamond-mining settlement into a ghost town. Kolmanskop sprung up after the discovery of diamonds in 1908 and the fine double-storey house and casino are reminders of the inhabitants' opulent lifestyle. Mining operations ceased in 1931 and the last people left in 1956. Dunes have partly engulfed some of the buildings while sand continues to stream through broken doors and windows. Some of the buildings, such as the casino with its skittle alley, have been restored.

See Map F ★★

LÜDERITZ

Built on a rocky outcrop along the bleak Diamond Coast, Lüderitz owes its existence to its port and the discovery of diamonds at nearby Kolmanskop in 1908.

A number of well-preserved German colonial buildings serve as reminders of the history of this picturesque town. Among them is **Goerke House**, a fine example of the diamond palaces built in the early 1900s. Other prominent buildings include the **Felsenkirche** (*see* page 37), which dominates the skyline above the town, and the **Old Railway Station** (1914), with its interesting combination of building styles. In the **Altstadt**, the historic heart of the town, the impressive **Kreplin House** is in sharp contrast to the rows of semidetached cottages in Berg Street.

The **Lüderitz Waterfront** integrates the business centre and the waterfront. It features squares paved with granite cobbles and stone, craft stalls, shops, restaurants and offices. There is also a small tidal pool and a pier. A **yacht trip** on the gaff-rigged schooner, *Sedina*, provides a different perspective on Lüderitz.

There are numerous picturesque bays and coves on the **Lüderitz Peninsula** that can be explored, or you can take a long walk at **Agate Beach** north of the town. Guided trips to **Elizabeth Bay ghost mining town** (*see* panel, page 53) and the **Bogenfels**, a spectacular rock arch on the coast south of Lüderitz, are conducted.

See Map H–E4   ★★

WATERBERG PLATEAU PARK

North of the town of Okahandja the gently undulating landscape of central Namibia is interrupted only occasionally by low hills and mountains. The most prominent of these is the Waterberg with its lichen-encrusted orange cliffs that rise abruptly above the plains, east of Otjiwarongo. The lush green trees and ferns that thrive around the springs surfacing on the mountain slopes are in sharp contrast to the surrounding dull green acacia savanna.

Guided scenic drives are conducted from the rest camp onto the plateau and although the dense vegetation makes game-viewing challenging there is always a possibility of seeing game. Species you might come across include black and white rhino, giraffe, roan, sable, buffalo, kudu and eland. In the absence of much game, the spectacular scenery is ample compensation and the sundowner drive is especially popular. Ensure that you are dressed warmly as it can be very cold and windy on the back of the open vehicle.

There are a number of short **walks** from the rest camp, while visitors with more time on hand can set off on the **Waterberg Self-guided Trail**. The route meanders for some 50km (30 miles) across the plateau and takes four days to hike. Another option is the **Waterberg Wilderness Trail**, a guided trail that is conducted in the wilderness area on the plateau.

Battle of Waterberg
Two graveyards below the Bernabe de la Bat rest camp are a silent testimony to the pitched battles fought between the German troops and Herero soldiers on 11 August 1904. Heavy casualties were suffered on both sides and when the Germans, with their superior fire power, advanced on nearby Hamakari the following day the resistance of the Herero broke and they began to flee, setting in motion the genocide of the Herero people (*see* panel, page 8).

Other reminders of the German era are the ruins of the Rhenish mission station dating back to 1891 and the foundations of the stables used by the *Schutztruppe*. Built in 1908 to serve as a police station, the beautifully restored *Rasthaus* is now a restaurant.

Below: *Hikers on a hiking trail through the Waterberg Plateau Park.*

☘ *See* Map A–C2   ★

NAUKLUFT

Set on the edge of the Namib Desert, the Naukluft Mountains tower 1000m (3280ft) above the desert plains and dunes to the west. The mountains are a sanctuary to Hartmann's mountain zebra, while kudu, gemsbok (oryx), springbok, klipspringer, baboon and an interesting variety of birds also occur here.

The **Naukluft camp site** is accessible by sedan car, but the mountainous terrain can only be explored on foot, or in a four-wheel-drive vehicle. From the camp site on the banks of the river it is a short walk to the refreshing mountain pools (*see* panel, this page) higher upstream.

A number of **hikes** can be done in this area (*see* page 42). A deep, narrow ravine, where chains assist hikers in a difficult section, is a highlight of the **Olive Trail**, which takes between four and five hours to hike. The more demanding **Waterkloof Trail** leads to the plateau and passes a series of crystal clear mountain pools that are especially inviting on a hot day. The tough **Naukluft Hiking Trail** has two options – a four-day 58km (36-mile) route, or an eight-day 120km (75-mile) route.

Driving skills will be tested to the limit on the **Naukluft 4x4 Trail** with its steep ascents, narrow winding passes and rocky terrain. The rewards are great and there are numerous stunning views along the 72km (45-mile) route, which takes two days to complete.

Tufa Formations

Naukluft has several excellent examples of tufa formations, the most accessible being those at the pools in the Naukluft River, a 20-minute walk upstream from the camp site. Also known as fountain stone, or travertine waterfall formations, these porous limestone deposits build up around springs and rivers as the water, rich in calcium carbonate, evaporates.

Another impressive tufa formation can be observed from the C14 between Solitaire and Büllsport.

Opposite: *Duwisib Castle, a German-style fortress, was restored in 1991.*
Below: *Ballooning over the southern Namib, not far from Sesriem in the Namib-Naukluft Park.*

See Map A–C3 ★

DUWISIB CASTLE

Southwest of Maltahöhe the scenery is characterized by the rolling hills of the *Duwisiberplatte*. Nestling among the hills, Duwisib Castle blends in so well with its surroundings that it is only seen at the very last moment. The 22-roomed castle was designed by Willi Sander (who also designed Windhoek's three castles) for a German military officer, Captain Hansheinrich von Wolf.

Stonemasons, builders and carpenters (who came from abroad) began building in 1908 and the imposing castle was completed the following year. Except for the stone which was quarried nearby, all the building material was imported and had to be transported overland by oxwagon from Lüderitz.

The Von Wolfs furnished the castle with fine imported furnishings, family heirlooms and paintings which also had to be transported from Lüderitz. Captain von Wolf became renowned for his extravagant entertainment as well as for the horses that were bred on the farm.

In 1916, Von Wolf was killed in the Battle of the Somme in France and his wife never returned to the farm. The castle and 50ha (125 acres) of surrounding land were acquired by the state in the 1970s and restored in the 1990s. Some of the original furniture, paintings and Von Wolf's collection of swords and firearms can still be seen, and picnic and camping facilities are available.

The NamibRand Nature Reserve

Covering close to 200,000ha (495,000 acres), the NamibRand Nature Reserve is one of the biggest privately owned conservation areas in southern Africa. It adjoins the Namib-Naukluft Park in the west, and the landscape ranges from stunning sand dunes and vast open plains to rocky outcrops. The beautiful landscape is the main attraction, but the reserve is also home to herds of gemsbok, springbok and a multitude of small creatures.

Balloon flights (*see* panel, page 44) are offered from Camp Mwisho, while **Wolwedans Dunes Lodge** and **Wolwedans Dune Camp** (*see* page 62) offer luxury accommodation and scenic drives. Active guests can experience the desert by joining one of the excursions operated by **Tok Tokkie Trails** (*see* page 42), which includes sleeping out in the desert for one or two nights.

Above: *Windswept sand often covers the highway that links Walvis Bay and Swakopmund, Namibia's premier holiday resort.*

Tourist Office
☎ (064) 20-9170
🖥 www.walvisbay.com.na
✆ walvisinfo@iway.na

Walvis Bay Enclave
Walvis Bay has been of strategic importance ever since the port and its surroundings were annexed by Great Britain in 1878. In 1910 the enclave was incorporated into the Union of South Africa and over the next 82 years it was administered by the Administration of South West Africa and as part of the Cape Province. South Africa retained control over Walvis Bay when Namibia became independent in 1990 and the enclave was only re-integrated into Namibia on 1 March 1994.

🌼 *See* Map D	★

WALVIS BAY

The 35km (22-mile) stretch of road from Swakopmund to Walvis Bay ranks as one of the most scenic tracts of coast in the world, especially on a sunny day when the cream-coloured dunes, blue sky and the Atlantic Ocean's rolling waves create an incredibly beautiful scene.

Walvis Bay is Namibia's major port and the fishing and salt industries play an important role in the town and country's economy. Although there are few reminders of the town's early history, Walvis Bay has many other attractions.

Tens of thousands of flamingos, pelicans and migrant waders are attracted to the Walvis Bay Lagoon, the focal point of the **Walvis Bay Wetland**. The wetland also includes the saltworks and sandspit forming the western arm of Walvis Bay and ranks as one of the most important wetlands along the west coast of Africa. Summer is the best time for birding.

The fresh southwesterly wind creates near-perfect conditions for **water sports** such as boardsailing and kite surfing. Exploring the lagoon in **kayaks** is popular and offers the possibility of getting close-up views of dolphins and Cape fur seals.

Quad-biking trips are conducted in the dunes which also serve as a perfect launching pad for **paragliders**. **Sandboarding** is another option for adrenaline junkies and speeds of up to 80kph (50mph) are reputedly reached on the highest dune. For more information on **dune sports** *see* page 43.

See Map H–B3/B4 ★

SKELETON COAST

Early mariners feared the voyage along the stretch of Namib coast which later became known as the Skeleton Coast. Here they frequently encountered dense fog and had to battle strong currents and gale force winds. Beyond the bleak coastline lay an inhospitable and waterless tract of land, and running aground meant certain death.

Since the early days of sail, the Skeleton Coast has claimed countless shipwrecks, but the restless waves and corrosion have destroyed all but the scantest evidence. The intrigue and mystery surrounding the name Skeleton Coast have lured thousands of visitors over the years. Others have been attracted by its unspoilt wilderness atmosphere and spectacular landscapes which range from low hills and salt pans to plains and magnificent light-coloured dunes north of Torra Bay. Small herds of springbok and gemsbok (oryx) can sometimes be seen at the springs in the **Uniab Delta**. The excellent catches of galjoen and kabeljou (cob) that are landed by keen anglers are legendary.

Terrace Bay is only open to visitors with confirmed bookings, but visitors may travel on the proclaimed road between the Ugab and Springbokwasser gates. Permits can be obtained at the gate before 15:00 and the exit gate must be reached before 17:00.

The Skeleton Coast Concession Area north of the Hoarusib River can only be visited by joining a fly-in safari operated by Wilderness Safaris (*see* panel, page 47).

The Lure of Diamonds
In the 1960s diamonds were discovered at various places along the Skeleton Coast. The large mine dump and small heaps of gravel at Terrace Bay and the cement floors of the diamond sorting plant and mining camp at Toscanini (further south) are reminders of this era. Although the diamonds were of gem quality, they were small and occurred in small pockets that were widely scattered. This, together with the insufficient reserves, made mining uneconomical and mining had ceased by the time the Skeleton Coast Park was proclaimed in 1971. When prospecting for diamonds began at Toscanini in 2001, environmentalists expressed fierce opposition to the possibility of mining in the park.

Below: *The notorious Skeleton Coast, graveyard of a thousand ships.*

☆ See Map H–B/C4   ★

Desert-dwelling Elephants

Northwestern Namibia is home to one of only two populations of desert-dwelling elephants in the world. Namibia's population of some 600 elephants is, however, substantially larger than the Saharan population of Mali in North Africa. Although their feet are larger than those of other elephants and their body mass lower, they are not a subspecies. They move up and down the west-flowing rivers, obtaining food from the riverine vegetation and water from springs. They occasionally wander over vast distances, covering up to 80km (50 miles) between drinking places.

Maintain a respectful distance from them and do not agitate or annoy them. Also never camp near springs or water holes as this could prevent animals from drinking after walking long distances.

Below: *Desert-dwelling elephants in the dry Uniab river bed.*

SOUTHERN KAOKOVELD

Table-top mountains, conical peaks, deep river valleys and plains merge between the Ugab and Hoanib rivers to create a landscape of raw beauty. Popular tourist attractions such as the **Petrified Forest**, **Twyfelfontein** and the **Burnt Mountain** (*see* page 20) and **Sesfontein** are accessible along gravel roads that are usually well maintained. There are, however, numerous other tracks within this area that are only negotiable by four-wheel-drive vehicles.

This barren and inhospitable tract of land is home to one of the largest populations of the western subspecies of the black rhino in the world and the famous desert-dwelling elephants. Large herds of gemsbok and springbok can be seen when the plains are transformed into waving grasslands after heavy thunderstorms. Other species include giraffe, Hartmann's mountain zebra, kudu, spotted hyena and nomadic lions.

Attractions include the historic **Fort Sesfontein** (built in 1905–06 and now a lodge) and the picturesque **Ongongo Falls** which tumble into a crystal clear pool close to the settlement of Warmquelle. The Palmwag Concession south of the Hoanib River offers excellent possibilities for seeing black rhino and elephant. Named after the palm trees clustered around a spring in a tributary of the Uniab River, **Palmwag Lodge** is an excellent base for four-wheel-drive excursions. Elephant are frequent visitors to the spring and often amble through the camp site at night.

See Map H–A1/A2/B2   ★

NORTHERN KAOKOVELD

Bounded by the Hoanib River in the south, this region stretches northwards for some 260km (160 miles) as the crow flies to the Kunene River. A mosaic of sparsely vegetated plains, towering mountains and boulder-strewn hills, it has justly been described as Africa's last wilderness. Except for the **Himba** (*see* page 10) who live here, and adventurous travellers wanting to experience its raw beauty, few people venture into northern Kaokoveld.

Scenic highlights include the spectacular **Epupa Falls** (*see* panel, this page), the **Marienfluss**, a wide valley bounded by the Otjihipa and Hartmann mountains, and the adjacent **Hartmann's Valley**.

In the Hoarusib and Hoanib valleys there is a possibility of seeing the famed **desert-dwelling elephants** (*see* panel, opposite). You also chance coming across herds of gemsbok (oryx) and springbok, giraffe and smaller species such as black-backed jackal.

A four-wheel-drive vehicle is needed to explore the rugged tracks, and travellers must be self-sufficient in respect of fuel, food, water, camping equipment and basic spares. As tracks are not signposted, a good map is essential. There are **community-run camp sites** at Ruacana's Hippo Pool, Epupa Falls on the Kunene River, in the Marienfluss and at Purros.

Exciting **canoeing trips** (*see* page 45) down the Ondorusu Gorge in the Kunene River are operated from Kunene River Lodge. The rapids are a few kilometres east of Swartbooisdrift.

Above: *The cascading waters of Epupa Falls.*

The Epupa Falls

The Epupa Falls, 190km (118 miles) upstream from the Kunene River mouth, are one of the most spectacular sights in Namibia. Here a shelf of resistant rock interrupts the flow of the Kunene River, causing it to fan out into several streams and channels. The main fall is 36m (118ft) high and plunges into a gorge of 6m (6.5yd) wide. What makes Epupa so special, however, is the multitude of cascades and small waterfalls spread out across a rock shelf that is 457m (500yd) wide.

Plans to build a hydro-electric power plant at Epupa have been temporarily shelved as the Angolan government favours a site in the Baines Mountains further downstream.

Above: *The insel-berg of Spitzkoppe was formed by vol-canic activity and subsequent erosion.*
Opposite: *Lianshulu Lodge guests study wildlife from a raft on the Kwando River in East Caprivi.*

Spitzkoppe Camp Sites

Spitzkoppe is run as a community tourism project and facilities include thatched bun-galows with communal ablutions, basic camp sites with braai places and five camp sites each with a shade cover, toilet and bush shower. ✉ 29km (18 miles) off the main B2 highway between Okahandja and Swakopmund. From the B2, take the turn-off to Henties Bay (D1918 gravel) for 18km (11 miles). Access is possible by 2x4 vehicle. ☎ (064) 53-0879 🍴 Bar with cold drinks. 🚶 Local tour guides; guided walks can be arranged on request.

See Map H–C5 ★

SPITZKOPPE

Some 25km (15 miles) west of the town of Usakos a granite inselberg (island mountain), Spitzkoppe, rises 700m (2300ft) above the surrounding plains. The German name refers to the sharp peak of the Gross (Great) Spitz-koppe which is also known as the Matter-horn of Namibia.

The inselberg dates back some 120 mil-lion years, when granitic magma (molten matter) intruded into the overlying rock and solidified. Subsequent erosion removed the surrounding rock, leaving only the Gross Spitzkoppe, Klein (Little) Spitzkoppe and Pondok Mountains standing.

The Spitzkoppe was conquered in 1946 when mountaineers reached its peak after three earlier attempts. Since then there have been over 440 successful ascents to the summit, which is 1728m (5670ft) high. The easiest and most popular ascent fol-lows a route near the northeastern corner of the Gross Spitzkoppe.

The chain of outcrops east of Gross Spitzkoppe owe their name, **Pondok Mountains**, to their resemblance to the dome-shaped roofs of some African home-steads. A chain handhold on the eastern side of the outcrops provides access to the **Bushman's Paradise**, a delightful rock amphitheatre with an overhang decorated with rock paintings. This site, together with three other rock-painting sites and a spec-tacular natural **rock arch**, can be visited by hiring a guide.

See Map B–D2/E1   ★

CAPRIVI

The dense woodlands, lush riverine forests, rivers and channels of northeastern Namibia contrast sharply with the Namib Desert and the arid savanna landscape that characterizes much of the country.

At **Popa Falls**, some 200km (125 miles) east of Rundu, the Kavango River cascades over a series of small rapids. The rest camp here is an ideal base for day visits to the nearby **Mahango Game Park** with its large elephant population, especially during the dry season. The park is also a sanctuary to roan, sable, red lechwe, kudu, bushbuck and buffalo and, with a checklist of over 400 species, offers excellent birding.

East of the Kavango River lies the **Caprivi Game Park** which extends for nearly 200km (125 miles) to the Kwando River. Plans have been announced to deproclaim two settlements inhabited by San people and to incorporate the Mahango Game Park into what will be known as the Bwabwata National Park.

The Kwando River flood plains and adjacent woodlands attract a variety of game, including large herds of elephant, buffalo, impala, tsessebe and a healthy population of leopard. A four-wheel-drive vehicle is needed to explore the **Kwando Triangle** to the south of the main road where there is a camp site with facilities at **Nambwa**.

Adventurous travellers geared for travelling and camping in the wilds and in possession of the necessary maps and confidence can visit the **Mudumu** and **Mamili national parks**.

Birding in Caprivi
With a checklist of close to 450 bird species, or nearly 70% of the total number of species in Namibia, the northeast of the country is a birders' paradise. What makes the Caprivi even more attractive is the fact that over a quarter of the region's birds do not occur elsewhere in Namibia. Among the noteworthy species are several Okavango Delta 'specials' such as slaty egret, coppery-tailed coucal, swamp boubou and greater swamp-warbler. Other exciting species include wattled crane, brown firefinch, Pel's fishing owl, southern brown-throated weaver and Arnot's chat. Raptors are represented by over 38 species, among them the western banded snake-eagle and African hobby. Birding is best in summer when there is an influx of migrant species.

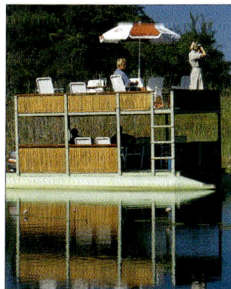

See Map H–F3 ★

Grootfontein's Alte Feste

The Alte Feste, or Old Fort, in Grootfontein was built as a military and administrative post in 1896. It was enlarged several times between 1900 and 1905 and became the office of a military magistrate after the occupation of South West Africa by South African troops in 1915. The limestone extension was added in 1922 and the building then served as a hostel for primary school children until the late 1960s. The fort subsequently fell into disrepair and after a public appeal it was saved from demolition and restored in 1974 to serve as a museum (*see page 37*). It was declared a national monument the following year.

Other reminders of Grootfontein's early history are the graves of several *Schutztruppe* in the cemetery alongside the town's main throughfare, and the Tree Park. The South West Africa Company (a mining company) established the park after Grootfontein became the seat of its headquarters in 1893.

Opposite: *The drought-resistant quiver tree, or kokerboom.*
Right: *Hoba, the largest single meteorite in the world.*

HOBA METEORITE

The Hoba Meteorite, west of Grootfontein, is the largest single meteorite in the world and its near cuboid shape makes it unique among meteorites.

The upper surface measures 2.95 x 2.84m (3.23 x 3.11yd) and its thickness varies from 75–122cm (30–48in). The meteorite consists of 82,4% iron, 16,4% nickel and 0,76% cobalt, as well as trace elements of carbon, zinc, copper, sulphur, chromium, iridium and germanium.

Its age has been estimated to be between 190 and 410 million years and it has been suggested that the meteorite broke up into several fragments before it struck the earth. Dating of a nickel isotope indicates that this took place less than 80,000 years ago. The meteorite was subsequently almost buried by a layer of calcrete which formed during a much wetter climate.

It was discovered in 1920 when a hunter, Jacobus Brits, scratched the rock with his knife and saw it glistening. It only became more widely known nine years later when a photograph was published in a newspaper.

See Map A–E4 ★

QUIVER TREE FORESTS

The name quiver tree is derived from the fibrous branches of the tree which were hollowed out by the San and used as quivers for their arrows. It is a characteristic species of the arid western regions of southern Africa, occurring from Namaqualand in South Africa's Northern Cape Province northwards to the Brandberg in Namibia's Erongo Region. The quiver tree is especially attractive between May and July when it is covered in bright yellow flowers. The average height is between 3m (10ft) and 5m (16ft), but it can reach a height of up to 9m (30ft) and become over 300 years old.

In southern Namibia quiver trees grow in such dense concentrations in a number of places that they almost resemble forests. Best known of these sites is the one on the farm **Gariganus**, about 15km (9 miles) northeast of Keetmanshoop. One of southern Africa's five species of tree aloes, the quiver tree usually grows singly and favours hillsides, rocky outcrops and mountain slopes, but here they grow among the black dolerite boulders.

An even larger concentration of quiver trees can be seen at **Garas Park**, about 20km (12 miles) north of Keetmanshoop. Adding to the allure of Garas are the dolerite boulders that have been fashioned into fascinating shapes. A ramble among the outcrops will reveal with only a little imagination a Herero woman with her headdress, a Land Rover, a pelican and a cannon.

Fossils

An interesting variety of fossils have been exposed on a farm some 40km (25 miles) northeast of Keetmanshoop. Most interesting of these is the well preserved fossil of a primitive aquatic reptile, *Messosaurus tenuidens*, which lived some 280 million years ago when the area was inundated by a shallow sea. The only such site open to the public, the fossils can be viewed by undertaking a guided 1km (0.6-mile) walk along the Fossil Trail. Also to be seen are some impressively large quiver trees and interesting dolerite formations. The grave of one of the German *Schutztruppe* killed in 1904 is of historical interest, while a short four-wheel-drive self-drive route will test driving skills.

Land of Contrasts

Wide-open spaces, large tracts of unspoilt wilderness, ever-changing landscapes, wildlife and a rich cultural heritage constitute the essence of a visit to Namibia. Small wonder then that Namibia is often referred to as the Land of Contrasts.

The **Namib Desert** with its stunning dunes, vast plains, mirages and silence is the top scenic attraction. Nearly five million hectares (12 million acres) of the desert enjoys the protection of the **Namib-Naukluft Park**, the third largest conservation area in Africa. Contrary to expectations, large areas of the park are surprisingly easily accessible from Swakopmund and Walvis Bay and can be explored by car and on foot (*see* page 18). **Sossusvlei** (*see* page 15) is one of the highlights of a visit to Namibia.

The **Kaokoveld** (*see* pages 28 and 29) in northwestern Namibia is a wilderness of rock, rugged mountains and deep river valleys. Popular tourist attractions in southern Kaokoveld are easily accessible, but there are innumerable rough tracks that can only be explored by four-wheel-drive vehicles. Upmarket lodges in remote locations cater for the luxury tourism market, while community-run camp sites (*see* panel) provide for the needs of do-it-yourself travellers.

Large perennial rivers, wetlands, riverine forests and lush teak woodlands in the **Caprivi** (*see* page 31) in northeastern Namibia combine to create scenery unlike anywhere else in Namibia. The arid southern reaches of the country provide a sharp contrast and from the viewpoints on the edge of the **Fish River Canyon** (*see* page 16)

Community Conservancies

Communities in communal areas were given the right to establish conservancies when legislation was adopted in 1996. The legislation enables the conservancies to use and benefit from wildlife on communal land, conduct trophy hunting and establish tourism facilities. **Nyae Nyae**, formerly Eastern Bushmanland, became the first communal area in Namibia to be declared a communal conservancy in 1998. Since then 28 other communal conservancies have been established throughout the country, while several others are still being planned.

Several communities have established **camp sites** and **craft centres** and offer the services of guides. Contact the **Namibia Community Based Tourism Association** (NACOBTA): ✉ Namibia Crafts Centre, Windhoek 🖥 www.nacobta.com.na

visitors will enjoy some of the most awe-inspiring vistas to be found in Africa.

When it comes to wildlife, the **Etosha National Park** (*see* page 14) is hard to beat. One of Africa's great conservation areas, it is a sanctuary to 114 mammal species, some 340 bird species and an estimated 50 different kinds of snakes. Three state-owned rest camps are located in the park, while luxury lodges and private reserves adjoin the park.

Other major proclaimed wildlife areas include the spectacular **Waterberg Plateau Park** (*see* page 23) and the parks in **Caprivi**. The minimal development of the region's parks allows visitors to experience wilderness at its best. Although the **Kaokoveld** is not a proclaimed conservation area it is home to the unique desert-dwelling elephant, black rhino, giraffe and herds of gemsbok and springbok.

Namibia's 19 state-owned parks, resorts and recreation areas account for just over 14% of the country's surface, while community conservancies (*see* panel opposite) cover over 71,000km^2 (27,400 sq miles). There is also an increasing number of private nature reserves.

For those interested in culture, options range from the rock art at **Brandberg** (*see* page 12) and **Twyfelfontein** (*see* page 20) to the ancient cultures of the **San** of Nyae Nyae and the **Himba** of northern Kaokoveld (*see* page 10). The German colonial architecture of **Swakopmund** (*see* page 19) and **Lüderitz** (*see* page 22) adds another dimension to the country's cultural heritage.

Namibia Tourism Board
Has information and brochures on tourist attractions, car hire and accommodation as well as maps.
☎ (061) 209-6000
🖳 www.namibiatourism.com.na
🖅 info@namibiatourism.com.na

Namibia Wildlife Resorts
Reservation and information office for the 22 state-owned resorts and camping sites under its management.
☎ (061) 23-6975
🖳 www.namibia-wildliferesorts.com
🖅 nwr@namweb.com.na

Opposite: *Sand dunes meet the cold Atlantic Ocean along the barren coast of the central Namib Desert.*
Below: *A herd of springbok, accompanied by a kudu, on the lookout for predators in Etosha.*

Below: *The historic whitewashed fort at Namutoni.*

Historic Buildings

Namibia's architectural heritage strongly reflects the German colonial building styles that were fashionable during the first decade and a half of the 1900s. Numerous buildings have been declared national monuments and are still in an excellent state of preservation. Although the largest concentration is in Lüderitz, Swakopmund and Windhoek, Tsumeb and Keetmanshoop also have some fine old buildings.

Architectural treasures in Swakopmund include the **old railway station building** (*see* panel, page 51), **Hohenzollern House** and **Woermann House** (*see* panel, page 50). Noteworthy of the architectural landscape of Lüderitz are the fine buildings representing the Art Nouveau or Jugendstil style. Among the town's striking buildings are **Goerke House**, **Kreplin House** and the **Altstadt** (old town) area (*see* page 22).

Given the conflicts between the German colonizers and Namibians, fortifications were built throughout the country. Several fine examples have survived, among which are the **Alte Feste** in Windhoek and in Grootfontein, **Fort Namutoni** in the Etosha National Park, and **Fort Sesfontein**.

In many instances German architectural styles were replicated in Namibia without adapting them to the local climatic conditions. **Erkraths Building** in Windhoek's Independence Avenue is a good example: its unusually steep pitched roof was designed to prevent snow from accumulating on top of the building!

Places of Worship

Christuskirche (Church of Christ)

Built as a place of worship for the German Evangelical Lutheran congregation of Windhoek, the Christuskirche was consecrated in 1910.

✉ *Fidel Castro Street, Windhoek,*
☎ *(061) 22-4294.*

Felsenkirche (Church on the Rocks)

This church, which dominates the skyline of Diamantberg (Diamond Mountain), was the first church to be built in Lüderitz for the German Evangelical Lutheran congregation.

✉ *Kirch Street, Lüderitz,*
☎ *(063) 20-2717.*

The German Evangelical Lutheran Church

Although a German Evangelical Lutheran Church congregation was established in Swakopmund in 1906, the church was only inaugurated in 1912. The architecture reflects the re-awakening of the baroque style in the Wilhelminische era (1884–94).

✉ *Daniël Tjongarero Street, Swakopmund,*
☎ *(064) 40-2574.*

Museums

Grootfontein Museum

Housed in the **Alte Feste** (old fort) dating back to 1896, the museum has reconstructions of a blacksmith's shop and a carpenter's workshop. It also has displays on the history of the town and area, as well as collections of cameras, typewriters and minerals.

✉ *Eriksson Street, Grootfontein,*
☎ *(067) 24-2456,*
🕓 *09:00–11:00 Wed, 16:00–18:00 (summer) and 15:00–17:00 (winter) Tue and Fri.*

Swakopmund Museum

The *People of Namibia* ethnographic exhibition is the focal

Sam Cohen Library

The Swakopmund Museum's reference section, housed in this library, has grown from a few donated books to more than 12,000. Pride of the library is the valuable 2000-title Africana Collection of Ferdinand Stich, which was donated to the Swakopmund Rotary Club in 1977. There are also newspapers dating from 1898 to the present, documents, historical photographs and maps. It is named after a prominent business personality, Sam Cohen, who financed the building. The library and the Swakopmund Museum are governed by the Society for Scientific Development, a non-profit-making body. The historic OMEG-Haus and the old Otavi station building also belong to the Society.

Above: *The National Art Gallery in Windhoek.*

Khorab
Khorab, just outside the town of Otavi, is where the German troops surrendered in 1915. This followed the invasion of the territory by South African troops, shortly after the start of World War I, in support of the Allied Forces.
   Prior to their surrender, the Germans dumped large quantities of ammunition and weaponry into Lake Otjikoto, northwest of Tsumeb. Several salvage operations have taken place since 1916 and among the weaponry recovered are cannons, gun carriages and ammunition wagons. Several thousand rifle and cannon rounds have also been brought to the surface. Many of the armaments were meticulously restored and are on display in the Khorab Room of the Tsumeb Museum.

point of the museum which also has displays on the early German colonial era, the natural history of the Namib Desert and an excellent mineral collection.
⊠ *Old Customs House, The Strand,*
☎ *(064) 40-2046,*
🕓 *10:00-13:00 and 14:00–17:00 daily.*

Tsumeb Museum

The museum has a collection of minerals from the Tsumeb Mine, displays on the town's history and traditional costumes. Cannons, machine guns, ammunition carriers and other items recovered from Lake Otjikoto are displayed in the Khorab Room (see side panel).
⊠ *Main Street, Tsumeb,*
☎ *(067) 22-0447,*
🕓 *09:00–12:00 and 14:00–17:00 Mon–Fri, 09:00–12:00 Sat.*

Keetmanshoop Museum

The early history of the town and region is depicted by a variety of displays housed in the historic **Rhenish Mission Church** which was inaugurated in 1895.
⊠ *Sam Nujoma Drive, Keetmanshoop,*
☎ *(063) 22-1256,*
🕓 *07:30–12:30 and 13:30–16:30 (16:00 on Fri) Mon–Fri.*

National Art Gallery of Namibia

The National Art Gallery has a permanent collection of over 2500 works of art. It includes paintings by explorer-artists, landscape and wildlife art, contemporary art and over 150 linocut prints by John Muafangejo (see panel, page 12). Displays are changed two or three times a year and temporary exhibitions of Namibian and international artists are held regularly.
⊠ *Robert Mugabe Avenue, Windhoek,*
☎ *(061) 23-1160 and 23-1391,*
🕓 *09:00–17:00 Tue–Fri, 09:00–14:00 Sat.*

Alte Feste Museum

The historic and cultural history sections of the State Museum is housed in the Alte Feste (Old Fort). Displays include the Namibian independence process, the country's national symbols, pottery, antique furniture and domestic implements. There is also a permanent exhibition on rock art.

✉ *Robert Mugabe Avenue, Windhoek,*
☎ *(061) 27-6817,*
🕑 *09:00–18:00 Mon–Fri, 10:00–13:00 and 15:00–18:00 Sat and Sun.*

Owela Museum

The natural history section of the State Museum has several small, but interesting dioramas of traditional activities such as fish culture in the northeast of the country, rope-making by the San (Bushmen) and the cultivation of mahango (millet) in the north. There are also displays of the country's fauna set against the backdrop of different areas.

✉ *Robert Mugabe Avenue, Windhoek,*
☎ *(061) 27-6822,*
🕑 *09:00–18:00 Mon–Fri, 10:00–13:00 and 15:00–18:00 Sat and Sun.*

TransNamib Museum

The history of railways and transport in Namibia is depicted in this museum located in the historic Windhoek railway station, built in 1912–13. Exhibits include a collection of office equipment, an old railway ticket counter and telecommunications equipment. Historical rail vehicles are displayed outside the museum.

✉ *corner Bahnhof Street and Mandume Ndemufayo Avenue, Windhoek,*
☎ *(061) 298-2186,*
🕑 *09:00–12:00 and 14:00–16:00 Mon–Fri.*

Owela

'Owela' is an indigenous name for a game of skill played in various parts of Africa where it is known under different names. It is usually played on a wooden board, or a stone slab with four rows of eight hollows each. Small pebbles, the kernels from stoned fruit, such as marula pips, or even balls of goat dung are placed in the hollows in the outside row and half of the hollows of the inside row on each player's side. They are then moved in an anticlockwise direction in accordance with the rules of the game; the aim of which is to capture as many of the opponent's stones as possible.

Below: *The Grootfontein Museum is housed in a historic fort.*

Windhoek Aloe

The Windhoek aloe (*Aloe littoralis*) is one of 26 aloe species occurring in Namibia. It is distributed throughout the country, but is especially prolific in the central parts. The Windhoek aloe belongs to the group of single-stemmed aloes and reaches a height of up to 3m (10ft). It is the emblem of the Windhoek City Council and their newsletter is appropriately named *Aloe*. In autumn, tubular red to pale red and yellow flowers are borne on candelabra-shaped inflorescences, adding a splash of colour to the surrounding landscape. The nectar of the flowers attracts bulbuls and mousebirds, as well as dusky, Marico and scarlet-chested sunbirds.

Below: *The green and pleasant landscape of the Daan Viljoen Game Park.*

Parks and Gardens
Daan Viljoen Game Park

Set among rolling hills bisected by deep valleys, Daan Viljoen Game Park protects 2700ha (667 acres) of landscape and scenery typical of the Khomas Hochland. Visitors can explore the park either along a 6km (3.7-mile) circular drive, two short day walks or a 32km (20-mile) hiking trail. Game includes red hartebeest, blue wildebeest, gemsbok (oryx), kudu, eland and Hartmann's mountain zebra.
✉ *18km (11 miles) west of Windhoek city centre on C28 to Swakopmund,* ☎ *(061) 22-6806,* ⏱ *daily, from sunrise to sunset.*

National Botanical Garden

Covering some 11ha (27 acres) on the ridge dividing the centre of Windhoek from Klein Windhoek, the garden contains Namibia's densest stand of the Windhoek aloe (*see panel*). A variety of plants can be seen along the footpaths.
✉ *can be seen to the north of Sam Nujoma Avenue from the city centre to Klein Windhoek, but access is along Orban Street,* ☎ *(061) 202-2011,* ⏱ *08:00–17:00 Mon–Fri.*

Zoo Park

With its lawns, trees, stream and fish pond, Zoo Park in the centre of Windhoek is much appreciated by residents and visitors. Except for the name, though, there is nothing to suggest that animals and birds were kept here until the zoo closed in 1932.
✉ *Independence Avenue, Windhoek,* ⏱ *daily, 24 hours.*

ACTIVITIES
Sport and Recreation

The Namibian coast is renowned for its excellent rock and surf **fishing** and offers world-class shark angling. Popular angling spots include the coast between Sandwich Harbour and Swakopmund, the National West Coast Recreation Area and Terrace Bay. Hardap and Von Bach dams offer good **freshwater angling** opportunities, while the Zambezi River in the northeast of the country is famous for its outstanding **tiger fishing**.

Popular destinations for **water-sport** enthusiasts include Walvis Bay Lagoon with its excellent conditions for boardsailing and kite surfing. Activities on the inland dams of Hardap and Von Bach include powerboating, water-skiing, boardsailing and yachting.

Swimming in the cold Atlantic sea water is only for the brave-hearted. However, swimming pools in the top resorts and rest camps offer welcome relief from the hot summer temperatures, while Ai-Ais, Reho Spa and Gross Barmen have outdoor thermal pools (*see* page 46).

Namibia is a popular **trophy hunting** destination and hunting is offered on game farms and big game hunting concessions in the remote northeastern regions of the country. Contact the Namibia Professional Hunting Association, ☎ (061) 23-4455.

Golf

The **Rossmund Golf Course** is one of the few desert courses in the world. It was designed by renowned South African golfer, Gary Player. The 18-hole course (6068m), with its water features and palm trees, lies on the banks of the Swakop River and is in sharp contrast to the surrounding desert. Springbok often visit and crop the fairways.

For a different golfing experience, along the coast there are 9-hole courses with sand fairways at Walvis Bay and Henties Bay. The latter has been laid out in an old course of the Omaruru River.

The **Windhoek Golf and Country Club** is set amid 72ha (178 acres) of savanna on the city's southern outskirts. The 18-hole course has 6199m (6780yd) of fairways. The club also has two bowling greens and tennis courts.

Golf Courses
Rossmund:
✉ 6km (3.7 miles) east of Swakopmund
☎ (064) 40-5644
Walvis Bay:
☎ (064) 20-9170
Henties Bay:
☎ (064) 50-0523
Windhoek:
☎ (061) 205-5223
📠 (061) 205-5220

Above: *Hikers negotiate the boulder-strewn river on the Fish River Canyon Hiking Trail.*

Fish River Canyon Hiking Trail

Starting at the northernmost viewpoint, the hike follows the meandering course of the Fish River for 85km (53 miles) to the Ai-Ais Hot Springs Resort. The terrain is demanding and ranges from large boulders and loose sand to round river stones and stretches of hard gravel. There are no facilities whatsoever and the hiking pace determines overnight stops. Hikers must be self-sufficient for the duration of the trail, which is usually hiked in four to five days. Owing to the dangers of flash floods and excessive summer temperatures, the route is only open from 15 April to 15 September, but even in midwinter temperatures can reach deep into the thirties. Book through Namibia Wildlife Resorts (*see* panel opposite).

Adventure Activities

Hiking

Heading the list of overnight trails is the renowned **Fish River Canyon Hiking Trail** (*see* side panel). The **Naukluft Hiking Trail** is a tough route with a circular 58km (36-mile) four-day hike, or a 120km (75-mile) eight-day option. In the **Waterberg Plateau Park** trailists can opt for a four-day self-guided hiking trail, or a guided wilderness trail, and there is the possibility of encounters with rhino, buffalo and other game. A guided trail is conducted in the environs of the **Ugab River**, the southern boundary of the Skeleton Coast Park. For more details, contact Namibia Wildlife Resorts (*see* panel, opposite page).

For an unparalleled experience of the Namib Desert, join an overnight guided desert walk offered by **Tok Tokkie Trails** in the NamibRand Nature Reserve (*see* panel, opposite page).

There are two day walks in the Namib section of the Namib-Naukluft Park (*see* page 18). The **Rock Sculpture Trail**, near Bloedkoppie, meanders past magnificent natural rock sculptures and is easily hiked in three hours. Set aside four to five hours for the **Tinkas Nature Walk**, near Middle Tinkas. Highlights include a desert fountain, an interesting geological formation and narrow rock tunnels through which one has to make one's way.

The **Olive Trail** (4 hours) in Naukluft (*see* page 24) partly follows a spectacular gorge with chains to assist hikers at a difficult spot. The **Waterkloof Trail** takes between six and seven hours to hike and features magnificent mountain pools near its end.

Dune Sports

The belt of coastal dunes between Swakopmund and Walvis Bay offers several adventure options. **Quad-biking** excursions along the Swakop River Valley and into the dunes opposite Long Beach Resort are popular. The route through the dunes is like a rollercoaster ride and opening up the throttle as you race up a dune is bound to get the adrenaline rushing. Split-second decisions and coordination are required to ensure that you do not become airborne as you crest the dune.

If you don't mind getting sand in your hair, eyes, ears, nostrils and mouth, try **sandboarding**. Lie-down boarding simply involves positioning yourself on a piece of hardboard that has been polished with wax. With the nose pointing down, lift your legs and the front of the board and slide down the dune slope. Speeds of up to 60kph (37mph) are reached on the highest dunes in the area. Stand-up boarding requires more skill as you 'surf' down the dune on a snowboard. Although not as fast as snow skiing, fairly high speeds can be reached, depending on the surface of the sand and the gradient of the slope. The only disadvantage is that once you've reached the end of the run you have to slog back up the dune.

The dunes opposite Long Beach Resort are a popular launching pad for **paragliding** and the fresh southwesterly breezes usually provide a good 'lift'.

Hiking
Namibia Wildlife Resorts
✉ Private Bag 13267, Windhoek
☎ (061) 23-6975
🖷 (061) 22-4900

Tok Tokkie Trails
✉ in the NamibRand Nature Reserve
✉ PO Box 162, Mältahohe
☎ (06638), ask for 5203

All Adventure Activities
Namib I
☎ / 🖷 (064) 40-4827

Quad-biking
Dare Devil Adventures
✉ based at Long Beach
☎ (064) 20-9532
🖷 (064) 20-9584

Outback Orange
✉ Swakopmund
☎ / 🖷 (064) 40-0968

Sandboarding
Alter Action
☎ (064) 40-2737

Below: *The magnificent dunes of the Namib sand sea.*

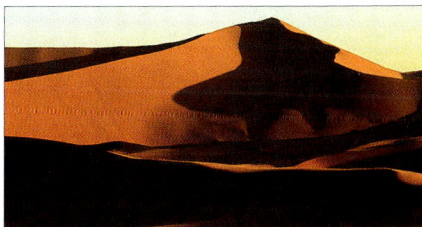

Ballooning
Namib Sky
Adventure Safaris
operate balloon flights
from the Sesriem area
and from Camp
Mwisho, further south
in the NamibRand
Nature Reserve. Take-
off is usually around
sunrise and as you drift
upwards on the ther-
mals, an awesome view
of the Namib Desert
slowly unfolds. From
the basket you have
uninterrupted 360°
views of the Namib
plains, punctuated by
isolated *inselbergen* or
'island mountains' and
the rolling red dunes of
the sand sea. The flight
lasts about an hour and
a hearty breakfast with
sparkling wine is served
in the middle of the
desert. ☎ (063) 29-
3233, ✆ (063) 29-3241

Below: *Negotiating
the rapids of the
Orange River in
a sturdy canoe.*

Taking to the Air

Atmospheric conditions at Swakopmund
are ideal for **skydiving** and adventure-
seekers can either do a one-day course, followed by a static jump from 915m (3000ft),
or opt for a tandem jump. The tandem
jump is made from 3050m (10,000ft) and
you freefall for 30 seconds at a speed of
220kph (135mph). When the instructor
opens the parachute at 1525m (5000ft) a
five-minute canopy ride takes you back to
earth. Whichever option you take will
reward you with a stunning bird's-eye view
of Swakopmund, the dunes and plains of
the Namib Desert to the east and the
Atlantic Ocean to the west. Contact **Ground
Rush Adventures** (*see* panel, opposite page).

Bitterwasser, about 250km (155 miles)
southeast of Windhoek, holds the most
international **soaring** records for any one
place in the world. It owes this distinction
to the clear skies, stable weather conditions
and excellent thermals that create ideal
conditions for the sport. The main soaring
season is from November to January, but in
addition to soaring a variety of other aerial
sports – such as microlighting, hot-air
ballooning and flying – are also pursued.
Contact Bitterwasser (*see* panel,
opposite page).

Microlight flights, operated
from Rag Rock near Twyfelfontein, provide a bird's-eye
view over the rugged landscape. Microlighting lessons
can be arranged with a
qualified instructor. Contact
Francolino Flyins (*see* panel,
opposite page).

Canoeing

In addition to canoeing the Orange River (*see* page 80), canoeing enthusiasts can also brave the rapids (and crocodiles) on the **Kunene River** which partly forms Namibia's northern boundary with Angola.

Above: *Descending into the dark subterranean depths of Gamkarab Cave, east of Outjo.*

Half-day trips on the **Ondorusu Gorge** are conducted from **Kunene River Lodge** which lies a few kilometres downstream of the gorge. A series of small, but exciting rapids are negotiated just below Ondorusu Falls, but the major challenge of the trip is shooting Birthday Chute. The lodge also conducts longer overnight trips for groups. A limited number of scheduled trips from just a few kilometres downstream of Ruacana Falls to Epupa Falls are conducted by **Felix Unite**, a South African company.

Caving

For those unafraid of venturing underground, two caves are easily accessible to the public, while several others will appeal to amateur speleologists.

Arnhem Cave, about 125km (78 miles) southeast of Windhoek, is the longest cave in the country and the length of the passages totals 4.5km (2.8 miles).

Exploring **Gamkarab Cave**, east of Outjo, involves a vertical 5m (16ft) descent down a ladder followed by a passage, 54m (60yd) long with a gradient of between 35° and 45°. The passage opens out into an enormous cave and an underground lake. Tours are offered at both caves and since there is no artificial lighting the caves are unspoilt.

Skydiving
Ground Rush Adventures
☎ (081) 124-5167

Aerial Sports
Bitterwasser
☎ (063) 26-5300
📠 (063) 26-5355

Microlight Flights
Francolino Flyins
☎ (067) 69-7041
📠 (067) 69-7042

Orange River Canoeing
Kunene River Lodge
☎ (065) 27-4300
📠 (065) 27-4301

Felix Unite River Adventures
☎ (+27 21) 670-1300
📠 (+27 21) 670-1400

Caving
Arnhem Cave
☎ (062) 58-1885
Gamkarab Cave
☎ (067) 31-3827 or
(067) 31-3386

Above: *The temperature of the thermal outdoor pool at Gross Barmen is about 29°C (52°F).*

The Camel Farm
☎ (064) 40-0363

Okakambe Trails
✉ Okakambe Farm
✉ PO Box 1668, Swakopmund
☎ (064) 40-2799
🖥 www.okakambe.com
📧 okakambe@iway.na

Gross Barmen Hot Springs
✉ Private Bag 2161, Okahandja
☎ (062) 50-1091
📠 (062) 50-1091

Ai-Ais Hot Springs
✉ Private Bag 2012, Karasburg
☎ (063) 26-2045
📠 (063) 26-2047

Reho Spa Recreation Resort
✉ Private Bag 1025, Rehoboth
☎ (062) 52-2774
📠 (062) 52-2769

FUN FOR CHILDREN

Namibia's vast open spaces, beaches and dunes provide a vast informal playground for children.

Facilities along the coast between Swakopmund and Walvis Bay include a tidal pool at Long Beach Resort and exciting super-tube rides at Dolphin Beach Resort. **Quad-biking** trips and **sandboarding** (*see* page 43) in the coastal dunes will thrill children with a sense of adventure. Another exciting option is to explore the Walvis Bay Lagoon in a stable **sea kayak** with Eco Marine Kayak Safaris (*see* page 52).

The Camel Farm, a few kilometres outside Swakopmund, offers short **camel rides**, while guided **horse-riding** outings along the Swakop River Valley are conducted by Okakambe Trails.

The **thermal outdoor pools** of the inland resorts of Gross Barmen (near Okahandja), Reho Spa (in Rehoboth) and Ai-Ais are a major drawcard. After a long drive the **swimming pools** at Etosha's three rest camps, the Waterberg Plateau Park's Bernabe de la Bat Rest Camp, Daan Viljoen Game Park, Hardap Dam, Sesriem and Hobas (near the main viewpoint overlooking the Fish River Canyon) are much appreciated on a hot summer's day. Children find the natural pools of Naukluft simply irresistible.

More serious-minded children can spend endless hours exploring the **museums** in Windhoek, Swakopmund, Grootfontein and Tsumeb (*see* pages 37–39).

NAMIBIA FROM THE AIR

Many of Namibia's most scenic landscapes are virtually inaccessible, or require extended journeys, often across difficult terrain, while some areas can only be explored by joining guided excursions.

Scenic flights from Swakopmund and Walvis Bay offer a bird's-eye view of some of the Namib's most spectacular attractions. The routes and distances vary, but among the highlights south of Swakopmund are Walvis Bay Lagoon, Sandwich Harbour, the beached wreck of the *Eduard Bohlen*, and Sossusvlei. Highlights north of Swakopmund include the Spitzkoppe, Cape Cross, the Brandberg and southern Kaokoveld. In Swakopmund, contact: **Pleasure Flights**, ☎ (064) 40-4500, and **Atlantic Aviation**, ☎ (064) 40-4749, and **Bay Air**, ☎ (064) 20-4319, in Walvis Bay.

Guests staying at the Cañon Lodge, Roadhouse or Mountain Camp (*see* page 60) can undertake scenic flights over the awesome Fish River Canyon, while Impalila Island Lodge (*see* page 59) offers scenic flights in the far northeast of the country.

Although Namibia's main gravel roads are generally in good condition, distances between tourist attractions are often vast. As a result, an increasing number of visitors are opting for flying. Although flying is expensive, travelling time is reduced significantly, leaving more time for enjoying the country. Several tour and safari operators offer camp-hopping itineraries which fly guests from one lodge or camp to the next. Among them is **Skeleton Coast Fly-in Safaris**, ✉ PO Box 2195, Windhoek, ☎ (061) 22-4248.

Skeleton Coast Concession

The Skeleton Coast concession, stretching from the Hoarusib River northwards, is only accessible to those joining a luxury safari operated by Wilderness Safaris. To minimize vehicular traffic and damage to the sensitive environment, guests are flown to their camp in the Khumib River Valley. From here day trips are undertaken to scenic highlights such as the spectacular clay castles of the Hoarusib, the roaring dunes and the Cape Fria seal colony. Viewpoints afford vistas of light orange dunes and dark plains merging to form scenes reminiscent of a marble cake. There is also a possibility of a rare encounter with the true desert elephants that roam the area. Contact **Wilderness Safaris**, ✉ PO Box 6850, Windhoek, ☎ (061) 27-4500.

Below: *The magnificent Clay Castles of the Hoarusib.*

Below: *The tall-steepled Christus-kirche viewed from Tintenpalast.*

Walking Tours
Exploring Windhoek on Foot

Zoo Park (map E–C3) in Independence Avenue is a convenient starting point for exploring the city on foot and offers an excellent view of the historic **Erkraths Building** (1910), **Gathemann House** (1913) and the **Hotel Kronprinz** (1902). A **stone sculpture** (*see* side panel) by renowned Namibian artist, Dörte Berner, marks the spot where elephants were killed about 5000 years ago. The nearby **Witbooi Memorial** (map E–C3) was erected in honour of the German soldiers killed in action against the Witbooi Nama in 1897.

Leave Zoo Park through the gate on its southern end, turn left, and walk up Fidel Castro Street. Just above the open parking area is the **Supreme Court** (the highest court in Namibia), and a short way on you pass **Ludwig von Estdorff House** (map E–D3). Built in 1891, it has served as a military canteen, a residence for the commander of the *Schutztruppe*, the National Library of Namibia, and now houses the British Council and the Namibia-German Foundation.

Overlooking the city, the **Christuskirche** (map E–D3) with its neo-Gothic and Art-Nouveau influences was consecrated in 1910. Immediately behind the church are the **Parliament Gardens** (map E–E3) with their statues of three of Namibia's leading figures in the struggle against colonialism. The imposing **Tintenpalast** (map

E–D3) was built in 1912–13 as offices for the German colonial government. Since independence it has served as the seat of the country's parliament.

To the south along Robert Mugabe Avenue, a larger-than-life statue, the Reiter Denkmal or **Rider Memorial** (map E–D3), attracts attention. It was unveiled on 27 January 1912 in memory of the German soldiers killed in the Nama and Herero Wars of 1903–07 and the 'Kalahari Expedition' of 1908.

Immediately behind the statue is the **Alte Feste**, or Old Fort. Built in 1890–91 to serve as the headquarters of the German *Schutztruppe*, it is the oldest building in the city. The historical section of the State Museum is housed here (*see* page 39).

Retrace your steps to the Christuskirche and then head north down Robert Mugabe Avenue past the **State House** (map E–D2). It was built in 1959 as residence and office of the South-African appointed administrator-general and since independence has served as residence and office of the president. A short way on is the **Owela Museum** (map E–D2) where the natural history section of the State Museum is housed.

Make your way to Independence Avenue and turn left (south), heading for the landmark **clock tower** (map E–C3), a replica of the corner tower where the Deutsche-Afrika Bank once stood. From here amble down **Post Street Mall** (map E–C3) with its arts-and-crafts vendors and its buildings reflecting the early German architectural style, to the **meteorite display** (*see* side panel).

Above: *Independence Avenue is Windhoek's main thoroughfare.*

Meteorite Display
The meteorites in Post Street Mall were collected at Gibeon, 200km (125 miles) south of Windhoek, in the early 1900s. They are fragments of a much larger meteorite which, in the distant past, broke up in the atmosphere. This resulted in the 'Gibeon Shower' over an area of 20,000km^2 (7720 square miles) – the largest known meteorite shower in the world. With a high iron content (91%), they are known as 'iron meteorites' – a feature that can be seen when looking at one that has been sawn in half. The meteorites also contain nickel (8%) and minute quantities of cobalt, phosphorus, chrome, copper and various trace elements.

Above: *State House, Swakopmund, formerly a magistrate's court.*

Woermann House

Woermann House, with its *fachwerkbau* (half-timbered style), stucco ceilings and panelled walls, is one of Swakopmund's most outstanding buildings. Originally known as Damara House, it was built as headquarters for the Damara and Namaqua Trading Company and completed in 1905. The building was later acquired by the trading firm of Woermann and Brock, and also served as a school hostel before it was restored to house the town library.

The **Damara Tower** served as a lookout post for ships and provides a bird's-eye view over the town – the key is obtainable from the library, or The Jetty gift shop in Am Ankerplatz.

Exploring Swakopmund on Foot

Three historic attractions are visible from the open space below Café Anton, making this a good starting point for a walk around Swakopmund. The **lighthouse** (map C–B2) dates back to 1902 when the lower stone portion was built. Originally built to serve as a magistrate's court, the **State House** (**Kaiserliches Bezirksgericht**), in front of the lighthouse, was completed in 1902. The **Marine Memorial** was dedicated to the First Marine Expedition Corps who took part in the suppression of the Herero Uprising of 1904.

Head south, past the craft vendors, up the stairs and follow Bismarck Street to its junction with Sam Nujoma Avenue. **Ritterburg**, on the right, was built as a residence for senior employees of the Woermann Shipping Line in 1906. Continuing along Bismarck Street you pass **Woermann House** (map C–B2) and the **Damara Tower** (*see* side panel), and still further on you reach the **Kaserne** (map C–B3). It was completed in 1906 to serve as barracks for the troops who built the original wooden jetty.

Turn left into Anton Lubowski Avenue and one block further turn left into Tobias Hainyeko Street to reach **Hohenzollern House** (map C–B3) – one of the finest examples of Victorian baroque in Swakopmund. Further on is the **Deutsche-Afrika Bank** (1909), while on the corner of Tobias Hainyeko Street and Sam Nujoma Avenue is the **Hotel Kaiserhof** which opened in 1905, but no longer serves this purpose.

Turn right into Sam Nujoma Avenue and walk three blocks up to Otavi Street where you reach the imposing **Villa Wille** (map C–C2) with its decorative corner tower. Here you turn left and at the corner of Otavi Street and Daniel Tjongarero Avenue you reach the **German Evangelical Lutheran Church** and the **Parsonage**. Directly opposite are the **old German government** and **municipal schools** dating back to 1913. Heading north along Otavi Street you soon reach the **old railway station** (*see* panel).

Retrace your steps to Daniel Tjongarero Avenue where you turn right, passing **Dr Schwietering House** (map C–C2) which was completed in 1910. A short way on you pass an old **advertising pillar** (1905) – the only genuine one remaining.

Situated diagonally across the street is the **Antonius Gebaude** which served as a hospital from 1908–1987. One block lower down is the old **Post Office** (1907) which now houses the town's municipal offices.

Ludwig Schröder House (map C–B2), on the corner of Theo-Ben Gurirab Avenue and Tobias Hainyeko Street, was built in 1903 as a residence for senior officials of the Woermann Shipping Line. Neighbouring **Altona House** (map C–B2) in Tobias Hainyeko Street was built in 1904–05 when the company needed additional accommodation. The window boxes and the *fachwerkbau* style of **Trend House**, opposite Altona House, gives this beautiful old building an almost Bavarian feel.

The Old Railway Station
Built in 1901, in a style locally known as 'Wilhelminischer Stil', the Swakopmund Station is one of the finest station buildings in southern Africa. The impressive clock tower did not feature in the original design, but was incorporated later by the architect Willi Sander. The building served as the terminus of the State Line until its closure in 1910, when the railway line from the rival Otavi Minen und Eisenbahn Gesellschaft was diverted to the State Station. In 1994 the area around the station was developed into a four-star hotel with the station as the focal point of the complex.

Below:
Hohenzollern House, one of the many graceful colonial buildings of Swakopmund.

Organized Tours & Activities

Companies based in Windhoek, Swakopmund and other major towns offer a variety of tours and safaris throughout the country. These range from luxury safaris for small groups to coach tours. Camping tours cater for those who prefer to rough it. Itineraries range from four or five days to 14 days, or longer.

Top destinations include **Sossusvlei** and the **Namib**, **Swakopmund**, **Etosha National Park**, **Twyfelfontein**, **Fish River Canyon** and **Lüderitz**. **Southern Kaokoveld**, more commonly referred to as Damaraland, is a popular camping safari destination.

Flying is a popular way of overcoming the long distances between destinations and several air charter companies and operators offer exclusive fly-in safaris to top lodges in remote areas.

From Windhoek

African Extravaganza has daily shuttles to Namib-Naukluft Lodge and Sossusvlei, scheduled safaris to Etosha and other destinations, and self-drive itineraries.

Face-to-Face Tours offer an interesting insight into life in Windhoek's Katutura suburb and the forced removals of 1959 (*see* page 17).

African Extravaganza
✉ PO Box 22028, Windhoek
☎ (061) 26-3082

Face-to-Face Tours
☎ (061) 26-5446

Kaokohimba Safaris & Tours
✉ PO Box 11580, Windhoek
☎ (061) 22-2378

Sense of Africa
✉ PO Box 2058, Windhoek
☎ (061) 27-5300

SWA Safaris
✉ PO Box 20373, Windhoek
☎ (061) 22-1193

Charley's Desert Tours
✉ PO Box 1400, Swakopmund
☎ (061) 40-4341

Eco-Marine Kayak Safaris
☎/📱 (064) 20-3144

Mola Mola
✉ PO Box 980, Walvis Bay
☎ (064) 20-5511

Rössing Mine
☎ (064) 40-2046 (Swakopmund Museum)

Swakop Tour Company
Contact George Erb at
✉ PO Box 1735, Swakopmund
☎ (064) 40-4088

Right: *An elephant observed on a game-viewing drive.*

Kaokohimba Safaris & Tours conduct tours focusing on the Himba and the magnificent landscape of northern Kaokoland.

Sense of Africa has scheduled coach and minibus tours covering the entire country, as well as a number of self-drive itineraries.

SWA Safaris in Windhoek have been conducting coach and minibus tours for over 50 years.

Above: *A guided tour of a ghost town makes an interesting excursion.*

From the Coast

Charley's Desert Tours in Swakopmund offer day tours into the Namib and overnight tours to wild and remote areas.

Eco-Marine Kayak Safaris offer trips in sea kayaks on Walvis Bay Lagoon, with a possibility of close-up views of dolphins and seals.

Mola Mola operates dolphin and seal cruises from the Walvis Bay Yacht Club. In addition to the possibility of seeing dolphins, whales are occasionally sighted and you are almost guaranteed good close-up views of Cape fur seals.

Rössing Mine, the largest open-cast uranium mine in the world, can be visited by joining a guided tour on the first and third Friday of the month. Book at the Swakopmund Museum.

Swakop Tour Company takes small groups on scenic natural history tours into the Khan and Swakop River canyons and the Namib dunes.

Elizabeth Bay

Elizabeth Bay, a ghost town south of Lüderitz, can only be visited by joining a half-day guided tour. Diamond mining started around 1911 and at one time it was the second-largest diamond mining town in the *Sperrgebiet*. Mining operations were interrupted by World War I and the Depression, and the mine was finally abandoned in 1948. Situated next to the ocean, the salt-laden mist and winds have eroded the unplastered walls into fascinating honeycomb patterns. Namdeb restarted mining operations in 1991 and visitors must make reservations at least four days in advance to get the necessary police clearance. Contact: **Ghost Town Tours** ☎ (063) 20-4031.

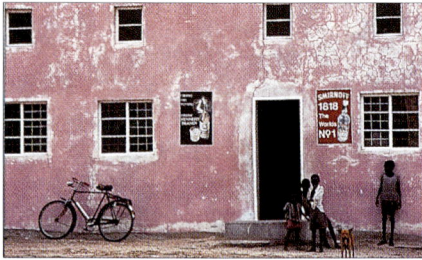

Namibian jewellery is renowned for its innovative designs inspired by the country's spectacular landscapes, wildlife and diversity of cultures. Local gemstones add to the uniqueness of each individually designed piece, which is crafted by highly skilled goldsmiths.

Tourmaline ranges from different shades of green (the most common) to pink, red and blue and features prominently in many pieces. Other popular gemstones include aquamarine, topaz, agate, dioptase and diamonds. Seed pods, ostrich eggshells, and traditional Namibian jewellery such as the *ekipa* buttons of the Owambo are incorporated into some pieces, giving them a distinctive African feel.

Windhoek and Swakopmund have a large number of top-class jewellers and prices compare extremely favourably with those in Europe.

Shopping In Windhoek
Bushman Art Gallery

Arts and crafts from Namibia and elsewhere in Africa are for sale, and there is also a fine private collection of weapons, musical instruments, jewellery and baskets of various Namibian cultural groups.
✉ *187 Independence Avenue,*
☎ *(061) 22-8828.*

Cape Union Mart

Sells a wide range of outdoor clothing, backpacks, sleeping bags, boots and other outdoor gear.
✉ *Maerua Mall,*
☎ *(061) 22-0424.*

Cymot

Popular with adventurous travellers, this shop sells camping equipment, motor accessories, tools and spares.
✉ *60 Mandume Ndemufayo Avenue,*
☎ *(061) 295-7000.*

Nakara

Designers and manufacturers of reversible Swakara (karakul) coats and jackets, ostrich-skin handbags, and leather belts.
✉ *165 Independence Avenue,*
☎ *(061) 21-5003.*

Rogl Souvenirs

This shop sells a wide variety of quality arts, crafts and souvenirs.
✉ *177 Independence Avenue,*
☎ *(061) 22-5481.*

Safariland Holtz

Stocks the largest selection of clothing for safaris, hunting, travel and leisure.
✉ *Shop 22, Gustav Voigts Centre, Independence Avenue,*
☎ *(061) 23-5941.*

The New Bookcellar

Specializes in Namibian books, and also sells German books and magazines

✉ *Carl List Haus, Fidel Castro Street,*
☎ *(061) 23-1615.*

Shopping in Swakopmund
Am Ankerplatz

A quaint shopping mall with a variety of interesting shops. Among them is African Kirikara Art, where you can buy hand-woven karakul carpets and hand-crafted jewellery.

✉ *Sam Nujoma Avenue,*
☎ *(064) 46-3146.*

Die Muschel

Sells paintings by Namibian artists and a wide selection of books on Namibia. Art exhibitions are held regularly.

✉ *Hendrik Witbooi Street,*
☎ *(064) 40-2874.*

Karakulia

The weavery sells hand-woven karakul carpets, rugs and wall hangings in a number of fascinating designs.

✉ *NDC Centre, Rakotoka Street,*
☎ *(064) 46-1415.*

Namib Stamps

Sells stamps and philatelic material from South West Africa to current issues.

✉ *Commercial Bank Arcade, Sam Nujoma Avenue,*
☎ *(064) 40-5560.*

Peter's Antiques

Sells antiques, books, coins, medals and domestic implements dating back to German colonial days. Also African artefacts.

✉ *24 Tobias Hainyeko Street,*
☎ *(064) 40-5624,*

Swakopmund Tannery

Famous for its veldskoene, a casual shoe made from kudu leather.

✉ *7 Leutwein Street,*
☎ *(064) 40-2633,*
📠 *(064) 40-4205.*

Swakopmunders

'Veldskoen' is an Afrikaans name for a handmade hide shoe worn by the pioneering white settlers. Today there are only a few factories left in South Africa that still make these shoes, and the Swakopmund Tannery is famous for its shoes. The uppers are made from the leather of the kudu, an antelope with magnificent spiral horns, and are stitched to a light rubber sole. The tannery, on the corner of Otavi and Leutwein streets, has been in operation since 1937. In addition to the famous Swakopmund 'vellies' (as these shoes are often referred to), sturdy leather boots, bags, purses and belts are also made here.

Best Buys

• **Kavango wood-carvings** from the Mbanguru Co-operative in Rundu.
• **Bushman handicrafts** from the San in eastern Bushmanland.
• **Zambian and Caprivian handicrafts** from Caprivi Art Centre.
• **Caprivian handicrafts** from Mashi Crafts at Kongola village.

Opposite: *A cuca shop in northern Namibia.*

Craft Markets
Namibia does not have the vibrant, colourful open-air markets that are so common in other African countries, but there are a number of markets where local arts and crafts can be bought. Some crafts sold at the Windhoek street markets are from northern Namibia, but many are from Kenya, Zambia, Zimbabwe and the Congo. Although bargaining is not as widely practised as in some countries, the initial asking price is usually higher than what you should pay.

Below: *Handicrafts on sale at the open-air market in Post Street Mall.*

Craft Markets
Namibia Crafts Centre, Windhoek

This outlet has the biggest selection of authentic and high-quality Namibian arts and crafts in the country. Articles on sale range from woodcarvings, pottery and basketry to embroidered linen, karakul rugs and jewellery. The **Craft Café** has an interesting menu that will appeal to the health-conscious. Exhibitions are regularly held at the **Omba Gallery**.

✉ *Old Brewery Building, Tal Street, Windhoek,*
☎ *(061) 24-2222,*
🕐 *09:00–17:30 Mon–Fri, 09:00–13:30 Sat (summer); 08:30–17:00 Mon–Fri and 09:00–13:30 Sat (winter).*

Post Street Mall Street Market, Windhoek

A variety of wood-carvings and domestic implements, basketry, masks and wire ornaments can be bought here.
✉ *Post Street Mall, Windhoek,*
🕐 *08:00–17:00 Mon–Fri, 08:00–13:00 Sat.*

City Bus Terminal Street Market, Windhoek

Tall wooden giraffes, woodcarvings, baskets and domestic imple-ments are sold.
✉ *Corner of Indepen-dence Avenue and Fidel Castro Street,*
🕐 *daily.*

Penduka Windhoek

Penduka, a name meaning 'wake up',

is a non-profit-making women's development project in Katutura, 12km (7.5 miles) from the city centre. Batik and embroidered table linen, duvets and cushions, hand-made by unemployed and rural women, are sold here. In the work-shop, you can watch the women sewing the needlework into finished products. A restaurant overlooks Goreangab Dam and there is also a tradi-tional village.

✉ *Dam Street, Katutura,*
☎ *(061) 25-7210,*
⏲ *08:00–17:00 Mon–Sat.*

Woodcarving Markets, Okahandja

The woodcarving markets in Okahandja, 70km (45 miles) north of Windhoek, offer exquisite carvings typ-ical of the north and northeast of the coun-try. Enormous carvings of hippos, giraffe and tall statues are pop-ular subjects. Carvings

fashioned out of tree roots and branches are also for sale. Some of the carvings are brought from the north already made, but you might also see craftsmen at work.

✉ *southern turnoff into Okahandja and the turnoff to Swakop-mund in Okahandja,*
⏲ *daily.*

Caprivi Art Centre, Katima Mulilo

A varied selection of high-quality pottery, basketware, wood-carvings and wooden domestic utensils from the Caprivi region and neighbouring Zambia and Zimbabwe are sold here. The first of its kind in rural Namibia, it has been in existence since 1988.

✉ *Katima Mulilo busi-ness centre,*
⏲ *daily, except Sun.*

Above: *Local art, handicrafts and African fashions are on display at the Caprivi Art Centre.*

Kavango Woodcarvers

The people of Kavango in northern Namibia have a long tradition of woodcarving for functional use. Bowls, spoons, mortars and other implements were fashioned for domestic use, but their skills also created a demand for commercial purposes. Many of the official buildings dating back to the South African colo-nial days were decorated with beautifully carved wall panels depicting ethnic-designed faces. Animal carvings, jew-ellery chests and replicas of aircraft used by the South African Air Force during the liberation struggle are also made. African teak (locally known as 'dolfhout') is mainly used, and with its beautiful pale brown to reddish brown heart-wood it ranks among the finest furniture woods in the world.

Above: *Fan palms look down on the reed huts at Palmwag Lodge.*

WHERE TO STAY

Hotel gradings range from one to four stars; one star being a standard hotel and four stars a superb hotel. There is currently no five-star grading. A **hotel pension garni** is a small private hotel (less than 10 rooms), which serves breakfast, but does not have to offer full restaurant facilities.

Lodges range from rustic thatch and reed structures to more conventional establishments offering *en-suite* rooms, or bungalows. **Luxury tented camps** are usually situated in remote concession areas, or private nature reserves. Their tariffs are generally inclusive of all meals and activities such as nature drives.

Gradings for **guest farms** (*see* panel) and **rest camps** range from one star (good) to three stars (excellent). **Bed-and-breakfasts** and **backpacker** establishments have mushroomed in Windhoek, Swakopmund and other major towns in the past few years.

The **Hospitality Association of Namibia** represents over 250 accommodation establishments from upmarket hotels and lodges to rest camps and bed-and-breakfasts. Members of the association maintain high standards of courtesy and hospitality. For more information, contact the **Hospitality Association of Namibia**, ✉ PO Box 86078, Windhoek, Namibia, ☎ / 📠 (061) 22-2904, ⌨ han@mweb.com.na

For information about community-run camp sites and craft centres in rural areas, contact **NACOBTA**, ☎ (061) 25-0558, or visit their office in the Namibia Craft Centre in Windhoek. Information can also be obtained from 🖥 www.nacobta.com.na

Cape Cross

• *LUXURY*
Cape Cross Lodge
(Map H–B5)
Right on the beach at
Cape Cross; all rooms
face the sea.
✉ *PO Box 259,
Henties Bay,*
☎ *(064) 69-4012,*
📠 *(064) 69-4013.*

Caprivi

• *LUXURY*
**Impalila Island
Lodge**
(Map B–H1)
Exclusive lodge re-
nowned for its out-
standing standards
and service.
✉ *PO Box 70378,
Bryanston 2021,
South Africa,*
☎ *(+27 11) 706-7207,*
📠 *(+27 11) 463-8251.*

**Lianshulu Main
Lodge and Bush
Lodge**
(Map B–F2)
Set on the banks of
the Kwando River
in the Mudumu
National Park.
✉ *PO Box 90391,
Windhoek,*
☎ *(061) 25-4317,*
📠 *(061) 25-4980.*

**Susuwe Island
Lodge** (Map B–E1)
Exclusive lodge on a
small island in the
Kwando River.
✉ *PO Box 70378,
Bryanston 2021,
South Africa,*
☎ *(+27 11) 706-7207,*
📠 *(+27 11) 463-8251.*

Namushasha Lodge
(Map B–F2)
On the banks of the
Kwando River, north
of Mudumu National
Park and overlooking
the Caprivi Game Park.
✉ *PO Box 6597,
Ausspannplatz,
Windhoek,*
☎ *(061) 24-0375,*
📠 *(061) 25-6598.*

Zambezi Lodge
(Map B–G1)
Hotel in Katima Mulilo
on the banks of the
Zambezi River.
✉ *PO Box 2862,
Windhoek,*
☎ *(066) 25-3203,*
📠 *(066) 25-3631.*

• *BUDGET*
**Popa Falls Rest
Camp**
(Map B–C2)
Self-catering wood
and thatch bungalows
at Popa Falls.
✉ *Namibia Wildlife
Resorts, Private Bag
13267, Windhoek,*
☎ *(061) 23-6975,*
📠 *(061) 22-4900.*

Etosha National Park

• *LUXURY*
Etosha Aoba Lodge
(Map H–E2)
Comfortable cottages
in a private game
reserve adjoining
Etosha National Park.
✉ *PO Box 1814,
Tsumeb,*
☎ *(067) 22-9106,*
📠 *(067) 22-9107.*

Mokuti Lodge
(Map H–E2)
Four-star hotel on a
private reserve on the
eastern boundary of
Etosha National Park.
✉ *PO Box 403,
Tsumeb,*
☎ *(067) 22-9084,*
📠 *(067) 22-9091.*

Mushara Lodge
(Map H–E2)
Ideally situated for
day trips into Etosha
National Park, 8km
(5 miles) further west.

Friendly atmosphere.
✉ PO Box 1814,
Tsumeb,
☎ (067) 22-9106,
📠 (067) 22-9107.

Ongava Lodge & Tented Camp

(Map H–D3)
Magnificent lodge and bush camp on private game reserve bordering Etosha.
✉ Wilderness Safaris, PO Box 6850, Windhoek,
☎ (061) 27-4500,
📠 (061) 23-9455.

• *BUDGET*
Etosha National Park's Rest Camps

(Map H–D3/E2)
Etosha National Park's three rest camps offer a variety of accommodation and camping.
✉ Namibia Wildlife Resorts, Private Bag 13267, Windhoek,
☎ (061) 23-6975,
📠 (061) 22-4900.

Fish River Canyon

• *LUXURY*
Cañon Lodge

(Map A–D5)
Rustic stone and wood bungalows that blend in with the granite outcrops.
✉ Cañon Travel Centre, P O Box 80205, Olympia, Windhoek,
☎ (061) 23-0066,
📠 (061) 25-1863.

• *MID-RANGE*
Cañon Roadhouse

(Map A–D5)
Individually decorated rooms built around a courtyard. Atmospheric Wheels Bar.
✉ see Cañon (above).

• *BUDGET*
Cañon Mountain Camp

(Map A–D5)
Self-catering with fully equipped kitchen, dining room and communal showers and toilets.
✉ see Cañon (above).

Ai-Ais Resort

(Map A–D6)
Luxury and standard flats with kitchens and bathrooms, huts with shared ablutions and camp sites. Indoor spa complex and outdoor thermal pool.
✉ Namibia Wildlife Resorts, Private Bag 13267, Windhoek,
☎ (061) 23-6975,
📠 (061) 22-4900.

Kaokoveld (South)

• *LUXURY*
Damaraland Camp

(Map H–B4)
Upmarket tented camp set in stunning surroundings in Central Damaraland.
✉ Wilderness Safaris, PO Box 6850, Windhoek,
☎ (061) 27-4500,
📠 (061) 23-9455.

Fort Sesfontein Lodge

(Map H–B3)
Comfortable rooms in the historic fort.
✉ PO Box 4896, Windhoek,
☎ (065) 27-5534,
📠 (067) 27-5533.

Mowani Mountain Camp

(Map H–C4)
The thatched dome-shaped roofs of the main complex echo their surroundings. Luxury tented accommodation.
✉ PO Box 40788,

Windhoek,
☎ *(061) 22-1994,*
📠 *(061) 22-2574.*

Palmwag Lodge

(Map H–B3)
Rustic reed and thatch
bungalows in Central
Damaraland, an area
renowned for desert-
dwelling elephant
and black rhino.
✉ *PO Box 339,
Swakopmund,*
☎ *(064) 40-4459,*
📠 *(064) 40-4664.*

Twyfelfontein Country Lodge

(Map H–C4)
Magnificent thatch-
roofed main complex.
Close to Twyfelfontein
rock engravings.
✉ *Namibia Country
Lodges, PO Box 6597,
Ausspannplatz,
Windhoek,*
☎ *(061) 24-0375,*
📠 *(061) 25-6598.*

Kaokoveld (North)
• *BUDGET*
**Kunene River
Lodge** (Map H–B1)
Camp sites and bunga-
lows on the banks of
the Kunene River,

47km (29 miles) west
of Ruacana town.
✉ *PO Box 643,
Ondangwa,*
☎ *(065) 27-4300,*
📠 *(065) 27-4301.*

Epupa Camp Site

(Map H–B1)
Magnificent camp site
under palm trees at
Epupa Falls. No
bookings.

Lüderitz
• *LUXURY*
Nest Hotel
(Map F–A2)
All the rooms in this
beachfront hotel
(including the restau-
rant and sunset bar)
have sea views.
✉ *PO Box 690,
Lüderitz,*
☎ *(063) 20-4000,*
📠 *(063) 20-4001.*

Hotel Zum Sperrgebiet

(Map F–B1)
In a quiet residential
area with expansive
views over the har-
bour and Lüderitz Bay.
✉ *PO Box 373,
Lüderitz,*
☎ *(063) 20-3411,*
📠 *(063) 20-3414.*

• *BUDGET*
Kratzplats
(Map F–A2)
Inexpensive B&B with
self-catering facilities.
✉ *PO Box 885,
Lüderitz,*
☎ / 📠 *(063) 20-2458.*

Namib-Naukluft Park
• *BUDGET*
(Map A–B1)
Camp sites with only
basic facilities but
spectacular settings.
✉ *Ministry of
Environment and
Tourism or Namib I
in Swakopmund,*
☎ *(064) 40-5476,*
📠 *(064) 40-3236.*

Naukluft
• *LUXURY*
**Büllsport Guest
Farm** (Map A–C2)
Offers magnificent
scenery and a variety
of outdoor activities.
✉ *Private Bag 1003,
Maltahöhe,*
☎ *(063) 69-3371,*
📠 *(063) 69-3372.*

• *MID-RANGE*
Zebra River Lodge
(Map A–C2)
Magnificent setting

in a canyon landscape with a variety of walks. Friendly atmosphere.
✉ *PO Box 11742, Windhoek,*
☎ *(061) 69-3265,*
📠 *(061) 69-3266.*

• **Budget**
Naukluft Camp Site (Map A–C2)
Shaded camp sites with hot showers; on banks of Naukluft River.
✉ *Namibia Wildlife Resorts, Private Bag 13267, Windhoek,*
☎ *(061) 23-6975,*
📠 *(061) 22-4900.*

Tsauchab River Camping
(Map A–C2)
Private camp sites with hot showers on banks of Tsauchab River, 30km (20 miles) south of Naukluft.
✉ *PO Box 221, Maltahöhe,*
☎ *(063) 29-3416,*
📠 *(063) 22-7011.*

Outjo
• **Mid-range**
Etosha Garten Hotel
(Map H–D3)
Comfortable accom-

modation, relaxed atmosphere and superb restaurant.
✉ *PO Box 31, Outjo,*
☎ *(067) 31-3130,*
📠 *(067) 31-3419.*

Sesriem and Sossusvlei
• **Luxury**
Kulala Desert Lodge & Kulala Tented Camp
(Map A–B2)
Three camps in a 21,000ha (52,000-acre) wilderness reserve; access to Sossusvlei.
✉ *Wilderness Safaris, PO Box 6850, Windhoek,*
☎ *(061) 27-4500,*
📠 *(061) 23-9455.*

Namib-Naukluft Lodge
(Map A–B2)
Comfortable accom-modation with great views over the desert.
✉ *PO Box 22028, Windhoek,*
☎ *(061) 26-3082,*
📠 *(061) 21-5356.*

NamibRand Nature Reserve
(Map A–C3)
Two upmarket estab-

lishments, Wolwedans Dunes Lodge and Wolwedans Dune Camp, set among the dunes in a private reserve bordering on the Namib-Naukluft Park.
✉ *PO Box 5048, Windhoek,*
☎ *(061) 23-0616,*
📠 *(061) 22-1020.*

Sossusvlei Lodge
(Map A–B2)
Accommodation in canvas and adobe-style units adjacent to Sesriem camp site.
✉ *PO Box 15109, Panorama, 7506, South Africa,*
☎ *(+27 21) 930-4564,*
📠 *(+27 21) 930-4574.*

Sossusvlei Mountain Lodge
(Map A–B3)
Exclusive lodge in the north of the Namib-Rand Nature Reserve; the ultimate in luxury.
✉ *Conservation Corporation Africa, Private Bag X7, Ben-more 2010, Johannes-burg, South Africa,*
☎ *(+27 11) 809-4300,*
📠 *(+27 11) 809-4400.*

Sossusvlei Wilderness Camp

(Map A–C2)

Thatched chalets with stunning desert views, each with a private plunge pool.

⌧ *Wilderness Safaris, PO Box 6850, Windhoek,*
☎ *(061) 27-4500,*
📠 *(061) 23-9455.*

• MID-RANGE

Betesda Guest Farm (Map A–C2)

Rooms with *en-suite* facilities and camping, 40km (25 miles) from Sesriem.

⌧ *PO Box 9385, Windhoek,*
☎ *(063) 69-3253,*
📠 *(063) 69-3252.*

• BUDGET

Sesriem

(Map A–B2)

Camp sites under the shade of ancient camelthorn trees, swimming pool and communal ablutions with hot water.

⌧ *Namibia Wildlife Resorts, Private Bag 13267, Windhoek,*
☎ *(061) 23-6975,*
📠 *(061) 22-4900.*

Shark Island

(Map F–A1)

Accommodation in the historic lighthouse and camp sites.

⌧ *Namibia Wildlife Resorts, Private Bag 13267, Windhoek,*
☎ *(061) 23-6975,*
📠 *(061) 22-4900.*

Skeleton Coast

• LUXURY

Skeleton Coast Camp (Map H–A2)

Exclusive tented camp in the Skeleton Coast concession area operated by Wilderness Safaris. Spectacular scenery.

⌧ *Wilderness Safaris, PO Box 6850, Windhoek,*
☎ *(061) 27-4500,*
📠 *(061) 23-9455.*

• MID-RANGE

Terrace Bay

(Map H–B3)

Basic bungalows. Tariff includes breakfast and dinner.

⌧ *Namibia Wildlife Resorts, Private Bag 13267, Windhoek,*
☎ *(061) 23-6975,*
📠 *(061) 22-4900.*

Swakopmund

• LUXURY

Swakopmund Hotel and Entertainment Centre

(Map C–C1)

Four-star hotel with the old railway station building as its focal point.

⌧ *PO Box 616, Swakopmund,*
☎ *(064) 40-0800,*
📠 *(064) 40-0801.*

Hansa Hotel

(Map C–B2)

Elegant four-star hotel with individually decorated rooms and personalized service.

⌧ *PO Box 44, Swakopmund,*
☎ *(064) 40-0311,*
📠 *(064) 40-2732.*

• MID-RANGE

Beach Lodge

(Map C–B1)

Stylish B&B on the beach, about 5km (3 miles) north of Swakopmund. All the rooms have sea views.

⌧ *PO Box 79, Swakopmund,*
☎ *(064) 40-0933,*
📠 *(064) 40-0934.*

Brigadoon B&B Cottages

(Map C–B1)

Tastefully furnished cottages and rooms; great hospitality; close to the main beach.

✉ PO Box 1930, Swakopmund,
☎ (064) 40-6064,
📠 (064) 46-4195.

Hotel Eberwein

(Map C–C2)

Small hotel in historic residence; sophisticated ambience.

✉ PO Box 2594, Swakopmund,
☎ (064) 46-3355,
📠 (064) 46-3354.

Hotel Europa Hof

(Map C–B3)

German atmosphere and hospitality, 200m from the beach.

✉ PO Box 1333, Swakopmund,
☎ (064) 40-5061,
📠 (064) 40-2391.

Hotel Pension Rapmund

(Map C–B2)

Good location; excellent value for money; this hotel has a homely atmosphere.

✉ PO Box 245, Swakopmund,
☎ (064) 40-2035,
📠 (064) 40-4524.

Sam Giardino's Hotel Pension

(Map C–D2)

Small stylish hotel; known for its outstanding hospitality and cuisine.

✉ PO Box 1401, Swakopmund,
✉ 89 Anton Lubowski Avenue,
☎ (064) 40-3210,
📠 (064) 40-3500.

Strand Hotel

(Map C–A1)

Overlooks Swakopmund's main beach with pavement café and restaurant overlooking the ocean.

✉ PO Box 20, Swakopmund,
☎ (064) 40-0315,
📠 (064) 40-4942.

Walvis Bay

• *LUXURY*

Burning Shores Beach Lodge

(Map D–A3)

On the beach at Langstrand. Dinstinctive African atmosphere, luxurious rooms and suites.

✉ PO Box 3357, Walvis Bay,
☎ (064) 20-7568,
📠 (064) 20-9836.

Lagoon Lodge

(Map D–A3)

Warm hospitality and tastefully decorated rooms overlooking Walvis Bay Lagoon.

✉ PO Box 3964, Walvis Bay,
☎ (064) 20-0850,
📠 (064) 20-0851.

• *MID-RANGE*

Langholm Hotel

(Map D–A1)

Comfortable rooms set around a beautiful garden. Great hospitality.

✉ PO Box 2631, Walvis Bay,
☎ (064) 20-9230,
📠 (064) 20-9430.

Protea Hotel Walvis Bay Lodge

(Map D–C1)

Ideal for business travellers, all rooms have internet connections. Fully equipped business centre.

✉ PO Box 30,

Walvis Bay,
☎ (064) 20-9560,
✆ (064) 20-9565.

Waterberg
• LUXURY
Waterberg Wilderness Lodge
(Map H–E4)
In the spectacular Otjosongombe Valley at the foot of the Waterberg Plateau.
✉ PO Box 767, Otjiwarongo,
☎ (067) 30-6303,
✆ (067) 30-6304.

• MID-RANGE AND BUDGET (CAMPING)
Bernabe de la Bat Rest Camp
(Map H–E4)
Rooms, bungalows, luxury bungalows and camping in a delightful setting below the Waterberg Plateau.
✉ Namibia Wildlife Resorts, Private Bag 13267, Windhoek,
☎ (061) 23-6975,
✆ (061) 22-4900.

Windhoek
• LUXURY
Hotel Heinitzburg
(Map E–E4)
Elegantly furnished in the style of the Heinitzburg Castle.
✉ PO Box 458, Windhoek,
☎ (061) 24-9597,
✆ (061) 24-9598.

Hotel Safari Court
(Map E–C4)
Four-star safari hotel; comfortable accommodation, 4km (2.5 miles) from the centre. Free city shuttle.
✉ PO Box 3900, Windhoek,
☎ (061) 24-0240,
✆ (061) 24-9300.

Kalahari Sands Hotel (Map E–C3)
City-centre hotel popular with business people and tourists.
✉ PO Box 2254, Windhoek,
☎ (061) 280-0000,
✆ (061) 22-2260.

Windhoek Country Club Resort & Casino (Map H–E6)
Four-star hotel with a tranquil setting and desert oasis theme on the southern outskirts of the city.
✉ PO Box 30777, Windhoek,
☎ (061) 205-5911,
✆ (061) 25-2797.

• MID-RANGE
Hotel Fürstenhof
(Map E–B2)
Well-known hotel situated about five minutes' walk from the city centre.
✉ PO Box 3320, Windhoek,
☎ (061) 23-7380,
✆ (061) 23-7855.

Hotel Safari
(Map E–C4)
Three-star hotel; comfortable, 4km (2.5 miles) from centre. Free city shuttle.
✉ PO Box 3900, Windhoek,
☎ (061) 24-0240,
✆ (061) 24-9300.

• BUDGET
Daan Viljoen Game Park
(Map H–E5)
Two-bed bungalows with communal ablutions (inclusive of breakfast); camp sites.
✉ Namibia Wildlife Resorts, Private Bag 13267, Windhoek,
☎ (061) 23-6975,
✆ (061) 22-4900.

Below: *The balcony of Windhoek's Gathemann's Restaurant overlooks Zoo Park.*

EATING OUT
What to Eat

Namibia's culinary tradition is largely derived from Germany and South Africa. However, top-class chefs are increasingly using seafood, Namibian game and delicacies like *omajova* and truffles to create a truly Namibian culinary identity (*see* panel, this page).

Many restaurants, especially in the coastal towns of Lüderitz and Swakopmund, specialize in **seafood**. **Black mussels** from Walvis Bay and **oysters** farmed at Swakopmund and Lüderitz are popular starters. **Rock lobster** from Lüderitz and calamari feature on some menus. Kabeljou (cob), a tasty fish with a firm texture, heads the list of line fish, while steenbras is also popular. Among the other fish dishes are smoked catfish, kingklip, sole and occasionally orange roughy, a fine-textured fish with a delicate flavour.

Large herds of free-ranging game provide a steady supply of healthy and superior-quality **venison**. Gemsbok (oryx), springbok and kudu are served either smoked, as pâtés, as steaks or in casseroles. Zebra, eland, warthog and crocodile are less frequently on offer. Lean and low in cholestrol, **ostrich** is a healthy red meat. Dishes range from smoked meat and carpaccio starters to steaks and ragout.

Since all livestock are reared entirely on natural grazing, Namibian meat is free of artificial stimulants and of a high quality. Prime cuts of succulent **beef**, especially steak, and veal are popular. The natural grazing gives **mutton** from the south of the country a distinctive aromatic flavour.

Traditional German fare includes *eisbein* (smoked pork shank) with **sauerkraut** (sour cabbage), and *kassler* (smoked pork chops). Some restaurants offer *telleressen* (literally 'plate meal').

Potjiekos, a typical South African dish, is essentially a stew prepared in a cast-iron pot over an open fire. **Biltong** (strips of air-dried beef or venison) and *droëwors* (dried sausage) are popular snacks.

The German baking tradition is still firmly established in Namibia, and German *backerei* are found in many small towns. *Brötchens* (the German equivalent of bread rolls) with a filling are a popular breakfast, or mid-morning snack. *Bauernbrot*, a farm-style bread, and *katenbrot*, a mixture of wheat and rye flour with sunflower seeds, are among the more than two dozen varieties of German-style bread. Three different types of grain are used in *dreikorn*.

The selection of mouth-watering cakes and pastries include **Schwartzwälder Kirschtorte** (Black Forest cake), **apfelstrudel** and **Sachertorte**, an Austrian speciality. German **stollen**, a rich fruit and nut loaf with a thin layer of marzipan, is popular at Christmas.

Above: *Potjiekos is prepared over coals.*

German-style Meat

A wide variety of sausages, polonies and other processed meats are made in the traditional German style. Among the typical German sausages is **bratwurst**, a frying or grilling sausage made from pork or veal. Despite its name, **bierwurst** (a Bavarian-style pork, beef and game sausage) does not contain any beer. **Jagdwurst**, or hunter's sausage, is made from pork and beef, while **käse griller** is a short sausage filled with Emmenthaler cheese. **Schinkenwurst** is a delicious ham sausage. Spreads include **zwiebeling**, made from liver and onion, and **teewurst**, a smoked pork meat spread.

Above: *Namibia Breweries only use pure ingredients.*

Namibian Drinks
Störtebeker is a uniquely Namibian schnaps. Weissenkorn is a clear wheat schnaps, while Doppelkorn, also a clear schnaps, is made from two types of grain and has an alcohol content of 43%. The flavoured range consists of Pamplemusen (grapefruit), Apfel (apple), Sauerer Apfel (sour apple), Walbeeren (forest berries), Wodka mit Feige (vodka with figs) and Pflaumen (plum). Maracuja is a passion-fruit spirit cooler. It is best served ice cold and can be enjoyed either as a short or a long drink with mixers such as soda, tonic water, or bitter lemon. Twenty-two different types of herbs are used in **Rittmeister**, a herbal liqueur similar to the well-known German equivalent, Jägermeister.

What to Drink
Beer

Namibia's beer drinking tradition dates back to the late 1800s with the arrival of German soldiers and officials. The imported German beer was, however, not suited to the hot and dry climate and at the beginning of the 1900s two breweries were established in Windhoek and another one in Omaruru.

After World War I the demand for beer dropped considerably and the Windhoek and Omaruru breweries amalgamated in 1920 to form South West Breweries. The brewery, on the corner of Sam Nujoma Drive and Tal Street, was in use until a modern brewery in Windhoek's Northern Industrial Area was commissioned in 1985. Soon after independence South West Breweries changed its name to Namibia Breweries.

'Namibia's favourite beer', **Windhoek Lager** (with an alcohol content of 4%) has a golden colour and mildly bitter taste. Slightly stronger (4.5%), darker and more bitter is **Windhoek Export**, a premium beer of international standard. **Windhoek Special**, the strongest of the lager beers (5.3%), has a deep golden colour and full-bodied taste.

Low in alcohol (2.4%), **Windhoek Light** was the first beer ever to be approved by the Heart Foundation of Southern Africa. It has 40% less carbohydrates than conventional beers, a crisp refreshing taste and is popular with those with an active lifestyle.

Urbock, a traditional 'Bock' beer, is a dark beer with a sweet taste and an alcohol content of 6%. It is available only during the

winter months when Namibians prefer a stronger beer and is usually drunk at room temperature.

Tafel Lager (4%) is a smooth, light lager beer, brewed by the Hansa Brauerei in Swakopmund. Established at the coastal town in 1929, it became part of South West Breweries after the company obtained the controlling interest in the Hansa Brauerei in 1968.

Brewed in accordance with the German Reinheitsgebot (Purity Laws), issued by the Duke of Bavaria in 1516, only the purest malted barley, hops, yeast and water are used. No grains or cereals (such as maize or rice) other than malted barley may be used and the process also prohibits chemical additives, stabilizers, sugar and preservatives. In conformity with the production standard the beer undergoes a traditional low temperature fermentation and maturation process of three to four weeks. Strict quality control measures are observed and samples are regularly sent to a leading German brewing institute to evaluate the quality.

Beer manufactured by Namibia Breweries compares favourably with some of the world's finest beers and has won several international awards.

Namibian Chocolate
The **Springer Schokoladenfabriek** in Windhoek is renowned for its fine chocolates. The liqueur-filled Cocktail Bar is especially popular, while chocolates with praline-flavoured centres, Weinbrand-bohnen (chocolate beans filled with brandy) and Knuspermischung (a chocolate and nut selection) are also manufactured here. A variety of marzipan products, seasonal specialities for Christmas and Easter, and hand-crafted chocolates are also produced.

Left: *Courtyard and sidewalk cafés offer outdoor dining opportunities in Windhoek.*

Kristall Wine Cellar
✉ 4km (2.5 miles) out-side Omaruru on the D2328
☎ (064) 57-0083
🕐 09:00–18:00 Mon–Fri, 09:00–13:00 Sat

Neuras Guest Farm
✉ PO Box 115, Maltahöhe
☎ / 📠 (063) 29-3417
🕐 by appointment

The Wine Bar
Offers a wide selection from 20 South African estate wineries (80 to 100 different wines), delicious light meals and magnificent views over the city. There ia also a wine shop.
✉ 3 Garten Street,
☎ (061) 22-6514,
🕐 17:00–23:00 Tue–Thu and Sun, 11:00–24:00 Fri and Sat.

Wine

Most wines featuring on the wine lists in restaurants are imported from South Africa. A fair selection of Portuguese wines is, however, available at Portuguese-run restaurants in Windhoek. Although the wines produced by the country's two cellars might not enjoy international acclaim, they are still worth trying.

The country's first winery was established in 1990 on the banks of the Omaruru River just outside the town of Omaruru. Four hectares (10 acres) have been planted under vines, and **Kristall Wine Cellar** pro-duces Cabernet Sauvignon, Cabernet Ruby and Colombard wines, as well as a lemon and a prickly-pear schnaps. Wine can be tasted in the tavern where delicious light meals can be enjoyed.

What started off as a hobby for Allen Walken-Davis when he planted the first vines on his farm south of the Naukluft Mountains in 1997 has developed into Namibia's second winery. The first wine under the **Neuras** label, Namib Red (a blend of Shiraz and Merlot), was released in 2002. Since the annual production is small, visits are by appointment only unless you stay at Neuras Guest Farm.

Below: *Kristall wines from Omaruru, where Namibia's first winery was established.*

Liqueurs and Schnaps

A variety of imported German liqueurs and schnaps is sold in bottle stores in Windhoek, Swakopmund and other major towns. **Barenjäger** is a rather sweet liqueur made with honey, while **Kirschwasser** is a clear schnaps made from cherries. **Ströh**, an Austrian rum, has an alcohol content of 80%.

Where to Eat

All major towns in Namibia have good restaurants, bakeries and cafés where fresh bread and light meals can be enjoyed. Hotels and state-owned rest camps serve breakfast, lunch and dinner. Windhoek offers a wide choice ranging from sophis-ticated restaurants with innovative Namibian and inter-national cuisine to steakhouses, franchise food outlets and takeaways.

Lüderitz

Nest Hotel

Seafood and interna-tional restaurant with superb ocean views.
✉ *Diaz Street,*
☎ *(063) 20-4000.*

On the Rocks

Seafood specialities.
✉ *Bay Road,*
☎ *(063) 20-3110.*

Okahandja

Okakango Restaurant

Indoor and terrace dining in a wildlife garden stocked with game.
✉ *northern outskirts of Okahandja,*
☎ *(064) 50-3280,*
📠 *(064) 50-3258.*

Outjo

Etosha Garten Hotel

Innovative menu featuring Austrian, Mediterranean and African dishes.
☎ *(067) 31-3130,*
📠 *(067) 31-3419.*

Swakopmund

Café Anton

Delicious German cakes, light lunches and à la carte dinners.
✉ *Bismarck Street,*
☎ *(064) 40-0331,*
📠 *(064) 40-5850.*

Cape to Cairo Restaurant

Authentic dishes from all over Africa are complemented by the distinctly African atmosphere.
✉ *Nathanael Maxuilili Street,*
☎ *(064) 46-3160.*

Erich's Restaurant

Excellent seafood dishes, as well as game and vegetarian.
✉ *21 Daniel Tjongarero Avenue,*
☎ / 📠 *(064) 40-5141.*

Kucki's Pub

Seafood specialities and meat dishes (the garlic steak is a house speciality).
✉ *22 Tobias Hainyeko Street,*
☎ *(064) 40-2407.*

Swakopmund Brauhaus

Casual atmosphere with a variety of local and imported beers. Traditional German food and Namibian game and fish dishes.
✉ *The Arcade, Sam Nujoma Avenue,*
☎ *(064) 40-2214,*
📠 *(064) 46-1055.*

The Tug

Large glass windows offer spectacular sunset views over the jetty and ocean. This restaurant spe-cializes in seafood.
✉ *at the jetty,*
☎ *(064) 40-2356,*
📠 *(064) 40-2356.*

Tiger Reef Beach Bar and Lapa

Set on the banks of the Swakop River, this open-air restaurant offers a wide variety of seafood dishes.
✉ Strand Street,
☎ (081) 244-0037 or 246-6774 (mobile),
📠 (064) 46-2597.

Walvis Bay

Crazy Mama's

Pizzas, pasta, seafood and meat dishes. Lively atmosphere.
✉ 133 Sam Nujoma Avenue,
☎ (064) 20-7364.

Raft Restaurant

Built on stilts on the edge of Walvis Bay Lagoon. Magnificent views and seafood.
✉ The Esplanade,
☎ (064) 20-4877,
📠 (064) 20-2220.

Willi Probst Bäckerei and Café

Renowned for its German Hausmannskost and German confectionery.
✉ 148 Theo-Ben Gurirab Street,

☎ (064) 20-2744,
📠 (064) 20-6908.

Windhoek

Abyssinian

Ethiopian meals served and enjoyed in the traditional way.
✉ 3 Lossen Street,
☎ (061) 25-4891.

African Roots

Variety of dishes with innovative names
✉ 5km (3 miles) from city centre on road to Hosea Kutako International Airport,
☎ (061) 23-2796,
📠 (061) 23-2790.

Bauern Stube

Extensive menu with German- and Austrian-style dishes. Generous portions at reasonable prices.
✉ Thorpe Street,
☎ (061) 25-7971,
📠 (061) 25-9833.

Café Schneider

This is a popular sidewalk café with an extensive, well-priced menu.
✉ Abe May Arcade (off Independence Avenue),

☎ / 📠 (061) 22-6304,
🕑 daytime only.

Café Zoo

Set on the edge of Zoo Gardens, this restaurant serves breakfast, innovative light lunches and delicious cakes.
✉ Zoo Park, Independence Avenue,
☎ (061) 22-3479,
🕑 closed evenings.

Cicada Café

Breakfasts, open sandwiches, salads, coffee and cake are served in the Wilde Eend Nursery.
✉ 10 Uhland Street,
☎ (061) 27-2632,
🕑 daytime only.

Dunes

Self-service buffet or à la carte menu.
✉ Kalahari Sands Hotel, Independence Avenue,
☎ (061) 280-0011,
📠 (061) 22-2260.

Fürstenhof

Excellent international and Namibian cuisine and service.

✉ *Dr Frans Indongo Street,*
☎ *(061) 23-7380,*
✆ *(061) 23-7855.*

Gathemann

Lovely views of Zoo Park from the balcony of historic Gathemann House.
✉ *175 Independence Avenue,*
☎ *(061) 22-3853.*

The Gourmet

Variety of international, game and fish dishes. Indoor or courtyard dining.
✉ *Kaiserkrone, Post Street Mall,*
☎ *(061) 23-2360,*
✆ *(061) 23-2882.*

Heinitzburg

Great views over Windhoek from the terrace, excellent cuisine and service.
✉ Heinitzburg Street,
☎ *(061) 24-9597,*
✆ *(061) 24-9598.*

Homestead

Restaurant with a homely atmosphere specializing in game, fish and vegetarian dishes. A selection

of fine wines is stored in an underground cellar.
✉ *53 Feld Street,*
☎ *(061) 22-1958,*
✆ *(061) 22-1846.*

Jenny's Place

Breakfasts and light meals served in a delightful garden setting. Gifts and crafts are for sale.
✉ *78 Sam Nujoma Drive,*
☎ *(061) 23-6792,*
🕐 *daytime only.*

Joe's Beerhouse

Open-air eatery with innovative décor, water features and open fires (in winter). Specialities include game dishes, spare ribs, steaks and *potjiekos.*
✉ *Nelson Mandela Avenue,*
☎ / ✆ *(061) 23-2457.*

Kokerboom

Delicious self-service buffet or à la carte menu.
✉ *Windhoek Country Club Resort,*
☎ *(061) 205-5911,*
✆ *(061) 25-2797.*

Luigi and the Fish

Extensive seafood menu with dining indoors or in the courtyard.
✉ *320 Sam Nujoma Drive,*
☎ *(061) 25-3699.*

O' Portuga

Portuguese cuisine, including a variety of seafood dishes, and good selection of Portuguese wines.
✉ *151 Nelson Mandela Avenue,*
☎ *(061) 27-2900,*
✆ *(061) 23-4423.*

Sardinia

Italian-run restaurant with a lively atmosphere and excellent pizzas, pasta, meat and seafood dishes.
✉ *Corner Independence Avenue and Garten Street,*
☎ *(061) 22-5600.*

Yang Tze Chinese

Popular Chinese restaurant catering for 'western' tastes.
✉ *351 Sam Nujoma Drive,*
☎ *(061) 23-4779,*
✆ *(061) 22-1191.*

Right: *Windhoek's College for the Arts is housed in a former school, built in 1911–12.*

ENTERTAINMENT
Nightlife

When it comes to nightlife, Namibians tend to be rather reserved. Soon after normal business hours the streets of Windhoek's central business district and other major towns are deserted. Weekend evenings are mainly spent socializing with friends, enjoying a drink at a bar, or chatting to friends at one of the numerous *cuca* shops (informal drinking places) in the outlying suburbs.

Music and Theatre

Although music is an integral part of the daily life of Namibia's indigenous cultural groups, especially in the rural areas, traditional musical performances are rare.

The Warehouse Theatre

The **Warehouse Theatre** is housed in Windhoek's Old Brewery Building which dates back to 1902 and was in use until 1985. The black walls with the original brewery piping and informal seating create a casual atmosphere. Drinks can be bought throughout performances and the theatre attracts a lively crowd. Plays, stand-up comedies, cabaret and live band and music performances feature regularly.

The Warehouse Theatre
⊠ Old Brewery Building, Tal Street, Windhoek
☎ (061) 23-4633
(Box office)

The National Theatre of Namibia
⊠ Robert Mugabe Avenue, Windhoek
☎ (061) 23-4633
(Box office)

The College for the Arts
⊠ Fidel Castro Street, Windhoek
☎ (061) 22-5841
℡ (061) 22-9007

The Franco-Namibian Cultural Centre
⊠ 118 Robert Mugabe Avenue, Windhoek
☎ (061) 22-2122
℡ (061) 22-4927

74

The National Theatre of Namibia

More formal cultural events, including drama, opera and concerts by the symphony orchestra as well as visiting international groups, are held at the National Theatre of Namibia.

The College for the Arts

The College for the Arts has regular music, ballet and modern dancing performances by lecturers and students.

The Franco-Namibian Cultural Centre

The Franco-Namibian Cultural Centre has a full programme of art exhibitions, workshops and French films. Concerts by local musicians are hosted here, and from time to time musicians from Central and West African French-speaking countries are brought to Namibia.

Gambling

Gambling was legalized in Namibia in 1994. Windhoek's Kalahari Sands Hotel, the Windhoek Country Club Resort and the Swakopmund Hotel and Entertainment Centre in Swakopmund all have casinos, but they are rather small and unlikely to appeal to visitors.

Jackson Kaujeua

Jackson Kaujeua is without a doubt Namibia's best known and one of the country's most popular musicians. He went into exile in 1973 and his liberation songs (beamed from neighbouring Angola by Swapo's Voice of Namibia) became well known in the north of the country. During his years in exile he played the guitar and sang in several countries, including England, France, the Netherlands and Sweden, to raise funds for the liberation struggle.

When he returned to Namibia in 1989 he received a hero's welcome. His music is influenced by his experiences during the years he was in exile and the Herero, Nama and Oshiwambo cultures. One of his most popular songs, *!Nubu !gubus*, was composed while he was in exile as a tribute to a girl from southern Namibia where he grew up.

Left: *The modern Franco-Namibian Cultural Centre offers a full programme covering various forms of art.*

Cycling

The Tour De Windhoek, the premier race for competitive cyclists in Namibia, is an international event held in October in Windhoek. The tour takes place over three days and in five stages. It is followed immediately by the Namibian Model Pick 'n Pay Cycle Classic, a fun cycle event with 30km (19-mile), 60km (37-mile) and 100km (62-mile) options. The Classic attracted over 1400 entries in 2002 and has boosted the interest in recreational and competitive cycling in Namibia. Both events are arranged by the **Namibian Cycling Federation**,
⊠ PO Box 20870, Windhoek,
☎ (061) 22-4725 or 24-4324,
✆ (061) 233207,
🖑 wpp@iway.na

Spectator Sports

Athletics

National and invitation championships are held at the Independence Stadium which has a tartan track.
⊠ *Rugby Street, Windhoek,*
☎ *(081) 124-4644.*

Cricket

The Olympia cricket field in Windhoek is the main venue for matches between local and visiting teams.
⊠ *Cricket Street, Windhoek,*
☎ *(081) 122-5551.*

Rugby

League matches are played at the Hage

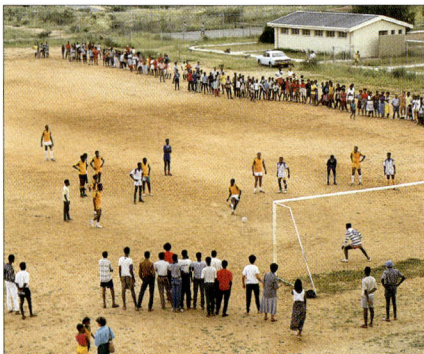

Geingob Stadium in Windhoek's Olympia suburb.
⊠ *Rugby Street, Windhoek,*
☎ *(061) 25-1717.*

Soccer

Soccer is the 'national sport' and matches are played throughout the country over weekends, often on fields without a blade of grass. International matches against teams from elsewhere in the region and Africa are played regularly in Windhoek.
⊠ *Independence Stadium,*
☎ *(061) 26-5691.*

Tennis

The Sport-Klub Windhoek (SKW) in Windhoek's Olympia suburb has several tennis courts and is the main venue for both recreational tennis and tennis championships.
⊠ *Sean MacBride Street, Windhoek,*
☎ *(061) 23-5521.*

Nightclubs, Bars & Discos

Chez-Ntemba

Located in the Windhoek city centre, Chez-Ntemba is where the 'in' and mature crowd dances away to the rhythmic beat of West and Central African music.

✉ *154 Uhland Street, Windhoek,*
☎ *(061) 25-3540,*
🕐 *most nights of the week.*

Club Thriller

Good African music is played at this lively club with its court-yard on Wednesdays and weekends. It also offers an all-night restaurant as well as secure parking.

✉ *Samuel Shikomba Street, Katutura,*
☎ *(061) 21-6669.*

La Dee Das

Lively disco where you can dance to a good mix of music, including R&B, pop, slow jam, hip-hop, rave, rock, African alternative and 70s and 80s oldies. This venue appeals to the 18–40 set.

✉ *Ferry Street.*

Pentagon Entertainment

Popular venue with the younger (18–40) generation. Music ranges from pop and rock to R&B and rave, and continues until the diehards finally leave. There are pool tables and outdoor seating.

✉ *Off Kepler Street, Southern Industria, Windhoek,*
☎ *(061) 22-8668,*
🕐 *Mon–Sat.*

Funkylab

Very lively bar where the young generation get together. Jazz band on Sundays. Breakfast and pub lunches served on weekdays and dinner in the evening.

✉ *Sam Nujoma Drive, /Ae//Gams Mall, Klein Windhoek,*
☎ *(061) 27-1964,*
🕐 *08:00–01:00 Mon–Sat, 16:00–00:00 Sun.*

Opposite:
Youngsters enjoy a game of soccer in Katutura, a township created under apartheid rule in the late 1950s.

Nightlife

Although Windhoek has a number of night-clubs, bars and discos, as well as local bands and musicians, it lacks the vibrant nightlife that is so characteristic of many African coun-tries. South African *kwasa kwasa* is often preferred to the rythmic *soukous* of DR Congo and the music from neighbouring Angola.

Most discos and nightclubs are only open on Wednesdays, Fridays and Saturdays and because of the legacy of apartheid, they tend to cater for different population groups.

Cuca **shops**, un-licensed bars similar to the shebeens in South Africa, are common throughout the north of the country and in Windhoek's Katutura township. The name (*cuca*) was originally adopted by shops near the Angolan border that sold Angolan beer of that name.

EXCURSIONS

In addition to exploring the popular tourist circuits, exciting excursions can be incorporated into visitors' standard itineraries. These unique excursions not only provide a different perspective of the country, but also open up areas that are otherwise inaccessible.

On the luxurious **Desert Express** (*see* opposite) you can sit back, relax and watch the transition of the landscape and vegetation from the central highlands to the plains and finally the dunes of the Namib Desert.

Although Namibia has few large rivers, the Orange River in the extreme south of the country is a popular **canoeing** destination (see page 80). No experience is necessary on the organized trips and even novices manage to negotiate the rapids fairly easily.

Experienced horse riders can tackle one of the toughest **horse trails** in the world operated by ReitSafari (*see* page 82). The same company also offers **camel trails** (*see* page 81) ranging from short excursions to overnight trails.

Regional tourism is rapidly gaining ground and an increasing number of visitors combine their Namibian holiday with some

Tok Tokkie Trails

Although at first glance the Namib Desert might appear to harbour little life, it is home to a multitude of fascinating plants and animals that are specially adapted to survive in their seemingly inhospitable surroundings.

Tok Tokkie Trails arrange guided overnight hikes into the desert from their base at Kwessiegat in the NamibRand Nature Reserve. The desert serves as a huge outdoor classroom and along the way visitors will gain an insight into various aspects of the desert. Nights are spent sleeping under the stars in comfortable camps set up by support staff, and a small day pack with water and lunch is all you need to carry.

For more information contact Tok Tokkie Trails, ☎ (06638), ask for 5203.

of the region's top tourist attractions in neighbouing Botswana and Zimbabwe. Regular scheduled flights link Windhoek with Maun, the gateway to the **Okavango Delta** in neighbouring Botswana. There are also regular flights between the capital and Zimbabwe's **Victoria Falls**, one of the world's greatest waterfalls (*see* page 83).

The Desert Express

The Desert Express is a unique rail experience which links the savannas of the central highlands to the desert coast and ocean. Inaugurated in 1998, the Desert Express ranks among the great train journeys of the world.

The train leaves Windhoek in the early afternoon and the first stop is made at **Okapuka Game Ranch**, about 30km (20 miles) north of Windhoek. Here guests are treated to close-up views of lions feeding, and can enjoy sundowners before boarding the train again. Drinks can also be enjoyed in the comfortable lounge and a gourmet dinner is served in the restaurant. The train then stops at a siding where guests can marvel at the magnificent night sky.

An early start is made the following morning and breakfast is served as the train slowly continues its journey across the spectacular Namib plains. The train's uniquely shaped large windows provide uninterrupted views of the magnificent scenery. On arrival at Swakopmund, guests are taken on an early morning walk in the dunes.

Accommodation on the Desert Express is provided in luxurious air-conditioned sleeper compartments with *en-suite* facilities. During the day the compartments convert into a private lounge.

The Desert Express
Location: Map H
Distance: 350km (217 miles) one way
☎ (061) 298-2600
📠 (061) 298-2601
🕐 twice a week in both directions.

Opposite: *Elephant are usually easily spotted in Khaudum Game Park, especially in the dry winter months when they stay close to water holes.*

Orange River
Location: Map A–D6
Distance from
Windhoek: 800km
(500 miles) south of
Windhoek

Felix Unite River
Adventures
☎ (+27 21) 670-1300
📠 (+27 21) 670-1400
💻 www.felixunite.co.za

Canoeing the Orange River

The Orange River, which forms Namibia's southern boundary with South Africa, is about 800km (500 miles) by road south of the capital. A number of companies based just downstream of the Noordoewer/ Vioolsdrif border post operate exciting canoeing trips throughout the year.

The relaxed pace allows canoeists to appreciate the barren, but spectacular landscape through which the Orange River has carved its way over countless aeons. Contorted rock strata, layered bands of rock and rugged mountains drift past slowly as you paddle your way downstream. There is also time to drift quietly up to kingfishers and other water birds attracted to the river and to explore the region's fascinating plant life.

Several rapids have to be negotiated and are bound to get the adrenaline rushing. However, they are all fairly easy to manage, even by novices, and the canoes are stable. Long stretches of 'flat' water between the rapids are excellent for relaxing – you can have a quick dip or even a water fight.

Below: *Brightly coloured canoes beached for the night on the banks of the Orange River.*

Lunches with fresh ingredients are served on the banks of the river. Nights are spent camping under the stars, and gourmet dinners are served around the campfire. The breakfasts are wholesome and nourishing.

The most popular trip ends at Aussenkehr and takes about four days to canoe at a leisurely pace. Longer trips on sections of the river downstream of Aussenkehr can be tailored for groups.

Camel Safaris

With its vast areas of desert it is not surprising that camels were used extensively by the police and the military in Namibia to patrol far-flung areas a century ago. With the advent of the motorcar they soon

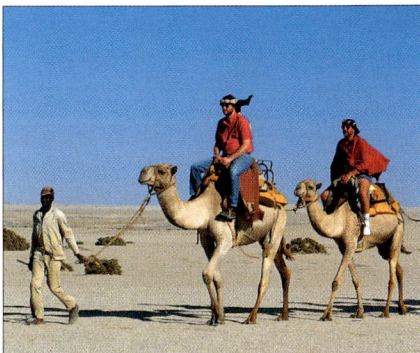

Above: *A leisurely camel trek is an unusual way to explore the desert.*

lost their utility, but some camels remained on farms in Namibia and South Africa.

In 1999 an enterprising couple, Lumpi and Waldi Fritsche, began offering overnight camel safaris through the Namib. From their base near Rostock Ritz Lodge, on the very edge of the Namib Desert, camel trails of up to four days are conducted. The route alternates between spectacular gravel plains punctuated by rocky hills, the orange dunes of the Namib and the Kuiseb River.

Daily distances depend on weather conditions and the fitness of the riders, but the pace is generally relaxed, with an extended break over midday. Since all personal and camping equipment is carried by the camels, trailists must be prepared to make do with only the bare basics, but this in itself is the very essence of the trail.

Camels, guides (English and German speaking), camel handlers, equipment and meals are provided. All trailists must provide are their own sleeping bag, ground sheet, ground pad, torch, water bottles, plate, mug, cutlery and soft or alcoholic drinks.

ReitSafari Horse and Camel Trails
✉ Farm Hilton, Box 20706, Windhoek
☎ Office: (061) 25-0764
☎ Ranch: (061) 25-7465
📠 (061) 25-6300
🖥 www.reitsafari.com
📧 reitsafari@iway.na

Camel Trails
Location: Map A–B2
Distance: Camel trails start approximately 200km (125 miles) southwest of Windhoek.
☎ (061) 25-0991
📠 (061) 25-0992

Namib Horse Trails

The 12-day Desert Trail from the central highlands to Swakopmund conducted by ReitSafari has been ranked among the top adventure activities in the world.

From **Farm Hilton**, 65km (40 miles) southwest of Windhoek, the route takes riders across the undulating highlands to an altitude of 2000m (6560ft) above sea level, and down the escarpment to the **Namib-Naukluft Park**. This leg through the park meanders from the **Kuiseb Canyon** area across the Namib plains to the **Swakop River Valley**. The final section takes trailists along the valley with its myriads of eroded gullies right to the beach at **Swakopmund**.

Nine days are spent in the saddle and the total distance covered is close to 400km (250 miles). Nights are spent camping in the open or under canvas, and delicious meals are prepared over an open fire.

Experienced riders who have undertaken the **Desert Trail** can experience the raw beauty of **Damaraland** on a 12-day trail which includes 7½ consecutive days in the saddle. Although the riding is easier, this trail is strictly for those who can 'ride for their life' as there is a possibility of close encounters with black rhino and desert-dwelling elephant in potentially dangerous situations. Back-up support is provided along the way for both trails. Contact **ReitSafari** (*see* panel, page 81).

Botswana and Zimbabwe

Many visitors combine a trip to Namibia with two of Southern Africa's other highlights, the **Okavango Delta** in Botswana and the **Victoria Falls** in Zimbabwe. Both are access-

Namib Horse Trails
Location: Map A–B2
Distance: Horse trails start approximately 65km (40 miles) south-west of Windhoek.

ible by fully tarred roads from Namibia, but it is far quicker to fly. **Air Namibia** has regular flights to Maun (the gateway to the Okavango Delta) and Victoria Falls.

The Okavango Delta, Botswana

The **Okavango Delta**, the world's largest inland delta, is a mosaic of waterways, riverine forests, flood plains, grasslands and islands. Large herds of elephant and buffalo roam the wilderness, as do lion, leopard, giraffe, zebra, waterbuck, impala and other species. Remote camps cater for luxury upmarket tourists, while camp sites in the **Moremi Game Reserve** have basic facilities for 4x4 self-drive tourists.

The Victoria Falls, Zimbabwe

Few waterfalls in the world can match the awesome **Victoria Falls** in Zimbabwe. Here the Zambezi River cascades along its full width of 1708m (1868yd) into a chasm of up to 108m (354ft) deep. The spray from the falls sustains a rain forest that is in sharp contrast to the surrounding woodlands. Wild white-water rafting trips, elephant-back rides, bungi-jumping, helicopter and microlight flights are among the activities offered.

The Okavango Delta
Location: Map B–E3
Distance from Windhoek to Maun: 800km (500 miles) by road

The Victoria Falls
Location: Map B–I1
Distance from Katima Mulilo: 200km (125 miles) by road

Air Namibia
For flight information and reservations:
☎ (061) 299-6333
📠 (061) 299-6146

Below: *Only from the air can the true scale of Victoria Falls be fully appreciated.*

Above: *A 4x4 nego-
tiates a sandy track
in Khaudum. Winter
is the prime time to
visit as summer rains
result in muddy
tracks and tall grass.*

Safe Driving
When driving on
Namibian roads, bear
the following in mind:
• Keep an eye out for
kudu and warthog
alongside roads at dusk,
at night and at dawn.
• On gravel roads switch
your vehicle's head-
lights on if a vehicle
approaches from the
front or overtakes you.
• Never overtake on
a gravel road if dust
restricts your vision.
• Sand often accumu-
lates between the driv-
ing surfaces on gravel
roads. When overtak-
ing, reduce speed and
move across to the
right-hand lane; taking
care not to oversteer.
• Avoid braking too
hard as the vehicle
could skid and leave
the road.
• Never speed on gravel
roads; 100kph (60mph)
is the maximum speed.

Best Times to Visit

Namibia has become
a year-round tourist
destination, but the
cooler months (May to
Aug/Sep) are the most
popular time. Daytime
temperatures are
more bearable during
these months,
although tempera-
tures can drop below
freezing at night. The
incidence of malaria
is lower at this time.
Game-viewing is more
rewarding as the
game is forced to con-
gregate in the vicinity
of pumped water
holes, perennial
springs and perma-
nent rivers. Visibility
is much improved as
many trees shed their
leaves and the grass
has withered. The
cooler months are
also the best time to
explore the country
on foot. Most hiking
and wilderness trails
in state-owned parks
are closed from Mar/
Apr–Oct/Nov because
of the high summer
temperatures.
Although day walks
can be hiked through-
out the year, trailists
must take precautions
such as avoiding walk-
ing during the heat
of the day, wearing a
wide-brimmed hat
and applying sun-
screen frequently.
Always carry at least
two litres of water
per person and keep
water intake up. The
summer months pro-
vide an ideal escape
from the cold north-
ern hemisphere. Max-
imum temperatures in
the north and south
of the country fre-
quently reach the
high 30s (centigrade),
but the central high-
lands are a few de-
grees cooler. Evenings
throughout the coun-
try are usually balmy.
Except for the far
south, summer brings
the prospects of
much-needed rain and
spectacular afternoon
thunderstorms occa-
sionally bring relief
from the heat.
Despite high temper-
atures, summer does
have its rewards.
After good rains the
barren landscape is

transformed into lush green fields of grass and floral delights. Between Oct and Mar/Apr there is an influx of migrant birds, making this the most rewarding period for birding. Temperatures along the coast are moderate throughout the year and many Namibians flock to the coast in December to escape the high temperatures of the interior. A fresh south-westerly wind is dominant, but easterly winds can cause temperatures to rise up to 40°C (104°F) in winter. Fog occurs on average one in every three days and is most prevalent in Swakopmund between May and August. Thick banks of fog usually roll inland in the late afternoon, blanketing the coast overnight, but clearing around mid-morning. With average surface temperatures of 16–17°C (61–63°F) in summer few visitors,

and Namibians for that matter, brave the icy waters of the Atlantic Ocean. In December the water at Swakopmund is occasionally warm enough for a swim.

Tourist Information

The Namibia Tourism Board has offices in **Germany** (Frankfurt) ☎ (+49 69) 133-7360, ✆ (+49 69) 133-73615; **UK** (London) ☎ (+44 207) 636-2924, ✆ (+44 207) 636-2969; **South Africa** Johannesburg ☎ (+27 11) 327-1006, ✆ (+2711) 327-1020, Cape Town ☎ (+27 21) 419-3190, ✆ (+27 21) 421-5840; and **Windhoek** ✉ corner of Fidel Castro and Werner List streets, ☎ (061) 290-6000, ✆ (061) 25-4848.

Entry Requirements

Visitors must have a **valid passport.** Temporary residence permits of up to 90 days are issued on arrival. Nationals of the following countries are exempted from visa

requirements when visiting Namibia as bona fide tourists: SADC member countries, except DRC, Mauritius and Seychelles; EU member countries at 2002, except Greece; Australia, Brazil, Canada, Cuba, Iceland, Japan, Lichtenstein, Malaysia, New Zealand, Norway, Russian Federation, Singapore, Switzerland and the USA. Applications for visas can be made with the Ministry of Home Affairs, ✉ Private Bag 13200, Windhoek, Namibia, or the following diplomatic missions abroad: Angola, Belgium, Botswana, Cuba, Ethiopia, France, Germany, Nigeria, Russian Federation, Sweden, UK, USA and Zambia.

Customs

Duty-free allowances include personal effects, sporting and recreational equipment and the following consumables:

2 litres wine, 1 litre spirits, 400 cigarettes, 50 cigars, 250g cigarette or pipe tobacco, 250ml toilet water and 50ml perfume, as well as new clothing and goods not exceeding N$500 in value. On goods valued up to N$1000, over and above the duty-free allowance, visitors have the option of paying a flat-rate assessment of 20%. If this option is not exercised, or the value of the imports exceeds N$1000, full customs duty is payable.

Health

The only compulsory health requirement is a yellow fever inoculation if the journey to Namibia passes through a yellow fever area by any other means than a scheduled air service. Visitors must arrange their own travel and medical insurance.

Getting There

Namibia is easily accessible by air and road.

By Air: Air Namibia, the national carrier, has four return flights a week between Windhoek and Frankfurt. The airline also operates regular flights to South Africa (Johannesburg and Cape Town), Angola (Luanda), Zimbabwe (Victoria Falls) and Botswana (Maun). South African Airways and British Airways operated by Comair also serve the Windhoek-Johannesburg route with regular scheduled flights. All international and regional flights use the Hosea Kutako International Airport, 45km (28 miles) east of Windhoek. Taxis operate between the airport and the city. For flight information and reservations, contact **Air Namibia**, ☎ (061) 299-6333, **British Airways**, ☎ (061) 24-8528 and **South African Airways**, ☎ (061) 27-3340.

By Car: The original vehicle registration document, or a letter from the owner authorizing use of the vehicle together with a copy of the registration document, must be carried and produced at the request of the authorities. Vehicles entering through Namibian/South African border posts do not require a Police Clearance Certificate if the journey is confined to Namibia. The certificate must, however, be obtained in South Africa if you intend to continue from Namibia to Angola, Botswana, Zambia or Zimbabwe. Namibia is linked by tarred road to South Africa via the Ariamsvlei and Noordoewer border posts, as well as a number of gravel roads. The Trans-Kalahari Highway which starts in Walvis Bay provides a tarred link with Botswana through the Buitepos border post, while the Trans-Caprivi Highway provides a good tar connection to northern Botswana via Ngoma border post. A 33km (20-mile) gravel road which is usually in good condition links Divundu on the Trans-Caprivi Highway with the Mohembo border post in north-western Botswana.

Car Hire: All the major car hire companies have offices at the Hosea Kutako International Airport, as well as in Swakopmund and other major centres. Drivers must be at least 23 years old and in possession of a valid International Driving Permit. Owing to the risk of accidents on gravel roads, the excess on the insurance is high.

Avis: ⊠ P O Box 2057, Windhoek, ☎ (061) 23-3166.
Budget: ⊠ P O Box 1754, Windhoek, ☎ (061) 22-8720.
Hertz: ⊠ P O Box 90135, Klein Windhoek, ☎ (061) 54-0115.
Imperial: ⊠ P O Box 1387, Windhoek,

☎ +264 61 227103. Members of motoring organizations affiliated to the **AIT** can obtain maps and assistance with tow-in services and accommodation reservations from the **Automobile Association of Namibia**, ⊠ Ground Floor, Carl List Haus, corner of Independence Avenue and Fidel Castro Street, ⊠ P O Box 61, Windhoek, ☎ (061) 22-4201, ⌂ (061) 22-2446.

Filling stations with petrol and diesel are available throughout the country. Unleaded petrol is sold in all the major towns, but in remote areas only unleaded fuel might be available. In small settlements off main roads fuel supplies can be unreliable and may only accept cash.

What to Pack

Casual dress is the norm during the day, except in some up-market hotels and restaurants. For evenings, 'smart casual' dress is required and

Wild Animals and Safety
Some basic precautions will help to avoid dangerous encounters with wild animals that might lead to injury or death:
• Never get too close to potentially dangerous animals such as elephant, especially if they have calves.
• In the Etosha National Park you may only get out of your vehicle in rest camps, at toilet enclosures and designated rest spots.
• In areas where you may get out of your car never venture too far from your vehicle and stay alert at all times.
• Crocodiles make it unsafe to swim in the rivers in the north of the country. For the same reason do not venture too close to the water's edge and avoid walking in long grass of seasonally inundated areas.

Public Holidays
• New Year's Day (1 Jan)
• Independence Day (21 Mar)
• Good Friday
• Easter Monday
• Workers' Day (1 May)
• Cassinga Day (4 May)
• Africa Day (25 May)
• Ascension Day
• Heroes' Day (26 Aug)
• Human Rights Day (10 Dec)
• Christmas Day (25 Dec)
• Family Day (26 Dec)

in sophisticated establishments jeans, T shirts and slip-slops are not acceptable. During winter (May–Sep) late afternoon, overnight and early morning temperatures can be cold, so pack trousers, long-sleeved shirts, a jersey, jacket or anorak. Warm clothing is essential throughout the year at the coast where fog and fresh winds are common. During the hot summer months (Oct–Apr) loose-fitting cotton clothes, short-sleeved shirts, shorts, a wide-rimmed hat and raincoat are essential. A light jersey will come in handy for the occasional cool summer evenings. Loose trousers and long-sleeved shirts are useful on summer evenings, to reduce the chances of being bitten by mosquitoes, especially in the north. Remember to pack comfortable footwear with a good grip to enable you to explore the countryside.

Money Matters

Namibian currency is the Namibia dollar and has the same value as the South African Rand which is also legal tender. Namibian currency should be converted to foreign currency before leaving the country.

Banks: ⏰ 09:00–15:30 Mon–Fri and 08:30–11:00 Sat.

Credit Cards: All major credit cards (Visa, Mastercard, American Express and Diners') are generally accepted, but some guest farms and shops in rural areas only accept cash. Fuel cannot be bought with credit cards.

ATMs are available in Windhoek and all major towns and are linked to the international network for Visa and Mastercard.

Foreign Exchange: Foreign currency and travellers' cheques can be converted at Hosea Kutako International Airport and at banks and bureaux de change in Windhoek and all major towns.

Taxes: Valued Added Tax of 15% is payable on all goods and services and is usually included in the price. VAT for goods purchased in Namibia can be claimed back from the Customs and Excise office at the Ministry of Inland Revenue in Windhoek, ☎ (061) 209-2642.

Tipping

Tipping for good service is optional; usually about 10% of the price of a meal. When petrol attendants clean car windows, or check water and oil a tip of around N\$2 is the norm, while the recommended fee for car attendants is N\$2 an hour. It is also customary to tip porters and taxi drivers.

Transport

Air: Air Namibia has regular domestic flights from Eros Airport, 4km (2.5 miles) from the city centre, to Swakopmund,

Ondangwa, Mokuti, Katima Mulilo, Lianshulu, Lüderitz and Rosh Pinah.

Road: Namibia has an excellent road network and all the country's major towns are linked by tarred roads totalling over 5400km (3355 miles). The 43,000km (26,700-mile) network of gravel-surface roads is usually well maintained. Driving is on the left-hand side of the road. Speed limits, unless otherwise indicated, are 120kph (75mph) on major tar roads, 100kph (60mph) on major gravel roads and 60kph (37 miles) in urban areas.

The carrying of driver's licences is compulsory and overseas visitors must have an International Driving Permit. Drivers' licences issued in Botswana, Lesotho, South Africa, Swaziland and Zimbabwe are accepted.

The wearing of seat belts is compulsory.

Rail: Starline passenger rail services link most of the major towns in the country, but the trains are slow and 500km (300 miles) takes approximately 11 hours. Services operate between Windhoek and Swakopmund/Walvis Bay and from Windhoek south to Keetmanshoop, Ariamsvlei and Upington in South Africa. The service from Windhoek northwards link Okahandja, Otjiwarongo, Otavi and Tsumeb to the capital. There is also a passenger rail service between Windhoek and Gobabis.
☎ (061) 298-2482,
📞 (061) 298-2495.

Bus: Intercape Mainliner operates regular scheduled bus services between Windhoek and Walvis Bay and south from the capital to Keetmanshoop and Ariamsvlei border post continuing to Upington and Johannesburg. The northbound service to Victoria Falls is via Otjiwarongo, Tsumeb, Grootfontein, Rundu and Katima Mulilo.
☎ (061) 22-7847,
📞 (061) 23-3808.
TransNamib's Starline bus service operates between Keetmanshoop and Lüderitz. It also links several major centres to rural towns, villages and settlements.
☎ (061) 298-2482,
📞 (061) 298-2495.

Business Hours

Normal business hours are ⏰ 08:00/08:30–17:00/17:30 Mon–Fri and 08:00–13:00 Sat. Some shops have extended hours on Saturday afternoons and on Sundays. Most shops are closed on public holidays.

Time Difference

Namibian winter time commences at 02:00 on the first Sunday in April and is one hour behind South African Standard Time and one hour ahead of Greenwich Mean Time. Summer time commences at 02:00 on the first Sunday in

September and is the same as South African Standard Time and two hours ahead of Greenwich Mean Time. Border post times remain constant throughout the year, opening and closing in accordance with South African Standard Time. Summer time is applicable all year round in the Caprivi region.

Communications

The international country code for Namibia is +264. This is followed by the area code (Windhoek for example is 61 and Swakopmund 64) and the subscriber number. The ringing tone is a double ring which is repeated regularly, while the engaged tone is equal length on/off tones. When calling within the country, the Namibian area code must be preceded by a 0. Telephone cards can be bought from post offices and shops. **MTC**, Namibia's only

cellular network, provides coverage in all the country's major towns. It has roaming agreements with 150 mobile telecommunication networks in 66 countries.

Post offices: ⏱ 08:30–16:30 Mon–Fri and 08:00–12:00 Sat.

Electricity

The power system is 220/240 volts. Plugs are three-pin round; 15 amp outlets.

Weights and Measures

Namibia uses the metric system.

Health Precautions

As much as visitors appreciate Namibia's abundance of sunshine, caution should be taken against the harsh sun and **sun burn**. Wear a wide-brimmed sunhat and apply a high-factor sun protection cream frequently.

Although most visitors prefer to drink mineral water, **tap water** is safe to drink through-

out the country.

Malaria is endemic in the north and north-east of the country and the risk of contracting the disease is especially high during the rainy season (usually Oct–Apr). The malaria parasites have become increasingly resistant to prophylaxis and it is important to consult a doctor prior to leaving for Namibia. All **blood** is screened for hepatitis and AIDS by the Blood Transfusion Service of Namibia and is tested in accordance with internationally recognized standards. Namibia has an **HIV/AIDS** rate of just under 20% of the adult population, necessitating the necessary precautions. **Bilharzia** occurs in the backwaters and slow-flowing channels of rivers, as well as stagnant pools in the north and northeast of the country. Avoid drinking water, swimming or washing in these water bodies.

Pharmacies are available in all major towns. They are usually open during normal business hours, but some in Windhoek have extended hours. Private **doctors** in Windhoek are listed under 'Medical Practitioners' in the telephone directory. Windhoek has three private hospitals: Medi Clinic, ☎ (061) 22-2687, the Catholic Hospital, ☎ (061) 23-7237 and Rhino Park, ☎ (061) 22-5434. At the coast there is the Welwitschia Private Hospital, ☎ (064) 20-7207 in Walvis Bay and the Cottage Hospital, ☎ (064) 41-2200 in Swakopmund. Other private hospitals are the Medi Clinic in Otjiwarongo, ☎ (067) 30-3734.

Personal Safety

Like in most countries, tourists in Namibia are occasionally targeted by criminals. Despite an increase in crime involving tourists in recent years, it is seldom violent. The most common crimes are muggings involving money, jewellery, cameras and phones and car break-ins. As a rule it is fairly safe to walk around the streets of Windhoek, Swakopmund and other towns after dark, but avoid poorly lit and deserted streets. Do not carry large amount of cash and avoid wearing expensive jewellery. Valuables should be handed in for safekeeping at hotels. Luggage, equipment and shopping bags should be locked in the boot rather than being left where they could tempt someone to break into your car. In some rural areas petty thieving has become a problem. Do not leave camping gear and other valuables unattended; rather lock them away.

Emergencies

The national emergency number for the Police is ☎ 10111, while the numbers of ambulance services in major towns are listed in the telephone directory on the page preceding subscribers' numbers in the particalar town. International SOS, a worldwide organization, provides emergency medical and rescue services for its members, ☎ (061) 23-0505.

Etiquette

Namibians are conservative and topless sunbathing is illegal and frowned upon.

Language

English is the official language and is widely spoken, in addition to the national languages, although communication might be difficult in some remote areas. Afrikaans is spoken throughout the country, except in the Caprivi region. German is widely spoken, especially in shops in Windhoek, Swakopmund and Lüderitz.

INDEX OF SIGHTS

Name	Page	Map
Ai-Ais	16	A–D6
Alte Feste Museum	36	E–D3
Altona House	51	C–B2
Antonius Gebaude	51	C–B2
Bogenfels	22	A–B5
Burnt Mountain	20	H–C4
Bushman's Paradise	30	H–C5
Cape Cross	21	H–B5
Caprivi	31	B–D2
Caprivi Game Park	31	B–D2
Caprivi Art Centre	57	B–D2
Christuskirche	37	E–D3
Daan Viljoen Game Park	40	H–E5
Dr Schwietering House	51	C–C2
Duwisib Castle	25	A–C3
Elizabeth Bay	53	A–B5
Epupa Falls	29	H–B1
Erkraths Building	36	E–C2
Etosha National Park	14	H–D2
Felsenkirche	37	F–A2
Fish River Canyon	16	A–D5
Fort Sesfontein	36	H–B3
Gariganus	33	A–E4
German Evangelical Lutheran Church	37	C–C2
Gibeon Meteorites	49	E–C2
Goerke House	22	F–A2
Grootfontein Museum	37	H–F3
Gross Barmen	46	H–E5
Heinitzburg	36	E–E4
Hoba Meteorite	32	H–F3
Hohenzollern House	50	C–B3
Kaiserliches Bezirksgericht	50	C–B2
Kaserne	50	C–B3
Keetmanshoop Museum	38	G–A2
Kolmanskop	22	A–B4
Kreplin House	22	D–A2
Kristall Galerie	19	C–B1
Lüderitz	22	F
Ludwig Schröder House	51	C–B2
Ludwig von Estdorff House	48	E–D3
Mahango Game Park	31	B–C2
Marienfluss	29	H–A1
Moringa Forest	14	H–D3
Namibia Crafts Centre	56	E–C4
Namib-Naukluft Park	18	A–B1
NamibRand Nature Reserve	25	A–C3
National Art Gallery of Namibia	38	E–D2
National Botanical Garden	40	E–E4
National Marine Aquarium	19	C–A3
Naukluft	24	A–C2
Ongongo Falls	28	H–B3
Organ Pipes	20	H–C4
Owela Museum	39	E–D2
Popa Falls	31	B–C2
Post Street Mall Street Market	56	E–C3
Quiver Tree Forests	33	A–C4
Reho Spa	46	H–E6
Rider Memorial	49	E–D3
Rössing Mine	53	H–C5
Sam Cohen Library	37	C–C2
Sanderburg	36	E–E4
Schwerinsburg	36	E–E4
Sesriem Canyon	15	A–B2
Skeleton Coast	27	H–A3
Sossusvlei	15	A–B2
Spitzkoppe	30	H–C5
State House	49	E–D2
Swakopmund	19	C
Swakopmund Museum	37	C–A1
TransNamib Museum	39	E–C1
Tsumeb Museum	38	H–E3
Twyfelfontein	20	H–C4
Uniab Delta	27	H–B3
Villa Wille	51	C–C2
Walvis Bay	26	D
Waterberg Plateau Park	23	H–E4
Welwitschia Drive	18	H–C6
Windhoek	17	E
Witbooi Memorial	48	E–C3
Woermann House	50	C–B2
Zoo Park	40	E–C3

GENERAL INDEX

Page numbers given in **bold** type indicate photographs

A

Aba-Huab camp site 20
accommodation 58–65
advertising pillar 51
Agate Beach 22
Ais-Ais Hot Springs 16, 41, 46
Alte Feste Museum *see* museums & galleries
Alte Feste, Grootfontein 32, 37
Alte Feste, Windhoek 36, 49
Altona House 51
Altstadt 22, 36
Antonius Gebaude 51
Arnhem Cave 45
art 12–13
art galleries *see* museums & galleries
athletics 76

B

balloon flights 25, 44
banks 88
Battle of Waterberg 23
beer 66–67
birds 31
Bitterwasser 44
Bogenfels 22
Botswana 83
Brandberg 12, 35
Brits, Jacobus 32
Burnt Mountain 20, 28
Bushman Art Gallery *see* museums & galleries
Bushman's Paradise 30
Bushmen *see* San
business hours 89

C

Camel Farm 46
camel rides 46, 78, 81
canoeing 29, 45, 78, 80, **80**
Cão, Diego 7, 21
Cape Cross 7, 21, **21**
Cape fur seals 21
Caprivi 31, 34, 35
Caprivi Art Centre **57**
Caprivi Game Park *see* parks & reserves
carnival 11
castles 36
caving 45
children 46
Christuskirche *see* churches & cathedrals
churches & cathedrals
  Christuskirche 37, **37**, 48, **48**
  Felsenkirche 22, 37
  German Evangelical Lutheran Church 37, 51
  Rhenish Mission Church 38
City Bus Terminal Street Market 56
climate 6, 84–85
clothing 87–88
College for the Arts 74, 75
commemorations 11–12
communications 90
crafts 13, 56–57
cricket 76
cruises 53
cuca shops 54, 77
cuisine 64–65
currency 88
customs 85–86
cycling 76

D

Daan Viljoen Game Park *see* parks & reserves

Damara Tower 19, 50
Dead Vlei 15
Desert Express 78, 79, **79**
Deutsche-Afrika Bank 50
diamonds 27
Dr Schwietering House 51
drinks 66–68
driving 84
dune sports 26, 43
Duwisib Castle 25, **25**
duwisiberplatte 25

E

economy 9
electricity 90
elephants 28
Elizabeth Bay 22, 53
emergencies 91
Epupa Falls 29, **29**, 45
Erkraths Building 36, 48
etiquette 91
Etosha National Park *see* parks & reserves

F

fauna 6
Felsenkirche *see* churches & cathedrals
Fish River 16, **16**
Fish River Canyon 16, **16**, 34–35, 52
Fish River Canyon Hiking Trail *see* hiking trails
fishing 9, 41, **41**
flights 47, 52
flora 6
food *see* cuisine
Fort Namutoni 8, 14, 36, **36**
Fort Sesfontein 28, 36
fossils 33
Franco-Namibian Cultural Centre 74, 75

G

galleries *see* museums & galleries
gambling 75
game farming 9
game parks *see* parks & reserves
Gamkarab Cave 45
Garas Park *see* parks & reserves
gardens 40, 48
Gariep River *see* Orange River
Gariganus 33
Gathemann House 48
German Evangelical Lutheran Church *see* churches & cathedrals
ghost towns 22, 53
Gibeon Meteorites 49
Goerke House 22, **22**, 36
golf 41
government 9
Grootfontein 32
Grootfontein Museum *see* museums & galleries
Gross Barmen Hot Springs 41, 46
Gross Spitzkoppe 30
guest farms 58

H

Halali 14
Hardap Dam 41
Hartmann's Valley 29
health 86, 90–91
Herero 8, 11
Heroes' Acre 17
Heinitzburg 36
hiking 24, 42
hiking trails
  Fish River Canyon Hiking Trail 16, 42, **42**
  Naukluft Hiking Trail 24, 42
  Olive Trail 24, 42

hiking trails (cont.)
  Rock Sculpture Trail 18, 42
  Tinkas Nature Walk 18, 42
  Waterberg Self-guided Trail 23
  Waterberg Wilderness Trail 23
  Waterkloof Trail 24, 42
Himba 10, 35
history 6–9
Hoanib River 28, 29
Hoanib Valley 29
Hoarusib Valley 29
Hoba Meteorite 32, **32**
Hohenzollern House 19, 36, 50, **51**
holidays 87
horse riding 46, 78, 82
hot springs 46
Hotel Kronprinz 48
hunting 41

I

inselberg 18, 30

J

jetty 19
jewellery 54

K

Kaiserliches Bezirksgericht 19, 50, **50**
Kaokoveld 28–29, 34, 35, 52
karakul carpets 13
Kaserne 50
Katutura 17, 57
Kaujeua, Jackson 75
Kavango River 31
kayaking 46, 53
Keetmanshoop Museum *see* museums & galleries

Khoikhoi 7
Khorab 38
Klein Spitzkoppe 30
Kolmanskop 22
Kreplin House 22, 36
Kristall Galerie 19
Kunene River 29, 45
Kunene River Lodge 29
Kwando River 31, **31**
Kwando Triangle 31

L

language 91
lighthouse 19, 50, **50**
Lüderitz 22, 35, 52
Lüderitz Waterfront 22
Ludwig Schröder House 51
Ludwig von Estdorff House 48

M

Mahango Game Park *see* parks & reserves
Maharero, Samuel 8, 11
Maharero Day 11
Mamili National Park *see* parks & reserves
Marienfluss 29
Marine Memorial 50
markets 56–57
Matterhorn of Namibia *see* Spitzkoppe
Mbanderu 11–12
meteorites 32, 49
microlight flights 44
money *see* currency
Moremi Game Reserve *see* parks & reserves
Moringa Forest 14
Muafangejo, John 12, 38
Mudumu National Park *see* parks & reserves

museums & galleries see
Museum
Alte Feste Museum
39
Bushman Art Gallery
54
Grootfontein
Museum 37
Keetmanshoop
Museum 38
National Art Gallery
of Namibia 17, 38
Omba Gallery 56
Owela Museum 17,
39, 49
Swakopmund
Museum 19, 37–38
TransNamib Museum
17, 39
Tsumeb Museum 38
music 74–75

N
Nama 7, 8
Nambwa 31
Namib Desert 34, 34,
42, 52
Namibia Community
Based Tourism
Association 34
Namibia Crafts Centre
56
Namibia Tourism
Board 35
Namibia Wildlife
Resorts 18, 35, 43
Namib-Naukluft Park
see parks & reserves
NamibRand Nature
Reserve see parks &
reserves
Namutoni see Fort
Namutoni
National Art Gallery of
Namibia see
museums & galleries
National Botanical
Garden 40
National Marine
Aquarium 19

national parks see
parks & reserves
National Theatre of
Namibia 74, 75
nature reserves see
parks & reserves
Naukluft 24
Naukluft 4x4 Trail 24
Naukluft Hiking Trail
see hiking trails
Naukluft River 24
nightlife 74, 77
Nyae Nyae 34

O
Okahandja 11, 57
Okakambe Trails 46
Okapuka Game Ranch
78
Okaukuejo 14, **14**
Okavango Delta 78,
83
Old Fort see Alte
Feste
Old Railway Station
19, 22, 36, 51
Olive Trail see hiking
trails
Omaruru 12
Omba Gallery see
museums & galleries
Ondorusu Falls 45
Ondorusu Gorge 29
Ongongo Falls 28
Orange River 6, 78, 80
Organ Pipes 20
owela 39
Owela Museum see
museums & galleries

P
padrão 21, **21**
Palmwag Concession
28
Palmwag Lodge 28
paragliding 26, 43
parks & reserves
Caprivi Game Park
31

parks & reserves (cont.)
Daan Viljoen Game
Park 40, **40**
Etosha National Park
14, 35, **35**, 52
Garas Park 33
Mahango Game Park
31
Mamili National Park
31
Moremi Game
Reserve 83
Mudumu National
Park 31
Namib-Naukluft Park
18, 25, 34, 42
NamibRand Nature
Reserve 25, 42
Skeleton Coast Park
42
Waterberg Plateau
Park 23, **23**, 35, 42
Zoo Park 40, 48
Parliament Gardens
48
Parsonage 51
Penduka 56–57
people 10–13
Petrified Forest 28
Pondok Mountains 30
Popa Falls 31
post offices 90
Post Street Mall 49
Post Street Mall Street
Market 56

Q
quad biking 26, 43, 46
quiver tree forests 33,
33

R
Rasthaus 23
recreation 41
Reho Spa Recreation
Resort 41, 46
religion 10
reserves see parks &
reserves

restaurants 69–71
Rhenish Mission
   Church see churches
   & cathedrals
Rider Memorial **8**, 49
Ritterburg 50
rock art 7, 12, 20, **20**,
   30, 35
Rock Sculpture Trail
   see hiking trails
Rössing Mine 53
Ruacana Falls 45
rugby 76

S
safari 47
safety 87, 91
Sam Cohen Library 37
San 7, 35
sandboarding 26, 43,
   46
Sander, Willi 25, 36
Sanderburg 36
Sandwich Harbour **6**
Schutztruppe <I>8, 23
Schwerinsburg 36
sea kayaking 26
Sesfontein 28
Sesriem Canyon 15
shopping 54–57
shops 54–55
Skeleton Coast 27, **27**
Skeleton Coast Con-
   cession Area 27, 47
Skeleton Coast Park
   see parks & reserves
skydiving 44
soaring 44
soccer 76
Sossusvlei 15, **15**, 34,
   52
South West African
   People's Organiza-
   tion (Swapo) 8
Spitzkoppe 30, **30**
sports 26, 41, 43, 76
State House 49
Supreme Court 48
Swakop River Valley
   18

Swakopmund 19, 35,
   50–51, 52
Swakopmund
   Museum see
   museums & galleries
Swartbooisdrif 29
swimming 41, 46

T
tennis 76–77
theatre 74–75
Tikoloshe Afrika 13
time 89–90
Tinkas Nature Walk
   see hiking trails
Tintenpalast 48–49
tipping 88
Tok Tokkie Trails 25,
   42, 43, 78
Torra Bay 27
Toscanini 27
tour operator 52–53
tourism 9
tourist information 85
tours 52–53
TransNamib Museum
   see museums &
   galleries
transport 86–87,
   88–89
Trend House 51
Tsauchab River 15
Tsumeb Mine 38
Tsumeb Museum see
   museums & galleries
tufa formations 24
Twyfelfontein 12, 20,
   20, 28, 35, 52

U
Ugab River 42
Uniab Delta 27
Uniab River 28
Usakos 30

V
Victoria Falls 78, 83,
   83
Villa Wille 19, 51
visas 85

Von Bach Dam 41
von Trotha, General
   Lothar 8
von Wolf, Captain
   Hansheinrich 25

W
walks 23, 48–51
Walvis Bay 26
Walvis Bay Lagoon
   26, 41
Walvis Bay Wetland
   26
Warehouse Theatre
   74
Warmquelle 28
water sports 26, 41
Waterberg Plateau
   Park see parks &
   reserves
Waterberg Self-
   guided Trail see
   hiking trails
Waterberg Wilderness
   Trail see hiking trails
Waterkloof Trail see
   hiking trails
welwitschia 6, 18, **18**
Welwitschia Drive 18
WIKA 11
wildlife 6
Windhoek 17, **48**,
   48–49, **49**, 52
Windhoek aloe 40
wine 68, **68**
Witbooi Memorial
   48
Witbooi, Hendrik 8
Woermann House 19,
   36, 50
woodcarving 57

Y
yacht trip 22

Z
Zeraua Day 12
Zimbabwe 83
Zoo Park see parks
   & reserves